D1414978

POWER
and
EMOTION
in Infant-Toddler Day Care

SUNY Series in
Early Childhood Education:
Inquiries and Insights
Mary A. Jensen, Editor

POWER
and
EMOTION
in Infant-Toddler Day Care

Robin Lynn Leavitt

STATE UNIVERSITY OF NEW YORK PRESS

Published by
State University of New York Press, Albany

© 1994 State University of New York

All rights reserved

Printed in the United States of America

No part of this book may be used or reproduced
in any manner whatsoever without written permission
except in the case of brief quotations embodied in
critical articles and reviews.

For information, address the State University of New York Press,
State University Plaza, Albany, NY 12246

Production by Bernadine Dawes
Marketing by Dana Yanulavich

Library of Congress Cataloging-in-Publication Data

Robin Lynn Leavitt
    Power and emotion in infant-toddler day care / Robin Lynn Leavitt.
        p.   cm. — (SUNY series in early childhood education-
-inquiries and insights)
    Includes bibliographical references and index.
    ISBN 0-7914-1885-5 (hc). — ISBN 0-7914-1886-3 (pb)
    1. Day care centers. 2. Child care workers. 3. Children-
-Institutional care. 4. Early childhood education. I. Title.
II. Series.
HV851.L42 1994
362.7'12—dc20   93-28222
                                                           CIP

1 2 3 4 5 6 7 8 9 10

Dedication

To the children.

CONTENTS

Acknowledgments

What is an author? The coming into being of the notion
of "author" constitutes the privileged moment of *individual-
ization* in the history of ideas, knowledge, literature, philosophy, and the sciences.

—Foucault, "What is an author?"

Every text, being itself the intertext of another text, belongs
to the intertextual. . . .

—Barthes, "From work to text."

It is with great affection and appreciation that I acknowledge the contributions of the following individuals.

Words are inadequate to express the depth of my admira-
tion for and gratitude to Norman K. Denzin, always inspiring,
generous, and caring. Norman's work has had a profound influence on my scholarship. I have felt both nurtured and challenged
by Norman's interest in and attention to my work these past several years. His thorough critique of my draft forced me to rework
the project and without question contributed to the quality of the
manuscript.

Ralph Page has been one of my most demanding, and at
the same time, appreciative critics. Ralph presented me with continual challenges in a sincere spirit of conversation.

As my friend, colleague, and advisor, Daniel Walsh's suggestions and support have been very much appreciated.

It was in a political theory course with Belden Fields that
the original inspiration and ideas as to how to go about this project began to take shape, as I read both Foucault and Sartre. His
comments on a paper which served as the starting point for the
manuscript were invaluable.

Brenda Krause Eheart has been an interested, empathetic, and supportive friend throughout the years and particularly during the writing of this project.

Martha Bauman Power has been a supportive friend and colleague. She introduced me to the literature on emotions and interpretive theory, and generously shared her library.

Spencer Cahill provided me with a very helpful review of an early draft of this project, and directed me to read Goffman, whose insights added very much to my interpretations of the children's experiences.

I am very grateful to Carolyne J. White for her friendship, support, and appreciation and understanding of the disciplinary bridges I am trying to build.

I must also thank numerous students who shared their observations with me and from whom I learned so much.

Carolyn Casteel typed and repeatedly revised several versions of the text.

I must also thank the caregivers, who welcomed my students and me into their rooms, little knowing what sense I'd make of the experience.

I also wish to thank Priscilla Ross, my editor at SUNY, for her interest in and support of this endeavor, and J. Amos Hatch for his challenging and supportive review of the manuscript.

Finally, a special thanks to my parents, from whom I learned the challenges and rewards of noncomformity. Their lives and their unconditional love have given me the strength, courage, and fortitude to pursue an unconventional path.

I note here that portions of this text have been previously published and/or presented in the following forms:

(1991). Power and resistance in infant-toddler day care centers. In S. Cahill (Ed.), *Sociological studies in child development, vol. 4*, Greenwich, Conn.: JAI.

(1989). Emotional socialization in the postmodern era: Children in day care. *Social Psychology Quarterly* 52 (1): 35–43.

(1990, April). *The objectification of infants and toddlers in day care centers*. Paper presented at the Midwest Sociological Association annual meetings, Chicago.

1
Introduction

All reflection sets out from the problematic and confused.
—Dewey, *Experience and Nature*

This text is an investigation of the lived experiences of infants and toddlers in day-care centers, specifically as these experiences are problematic with regard to power and emotion in everyday interactions.[1] This project is also a philosophical exploration of the meanings of emotionally responsive, empowering child care in group settings. In the process of setting forth an account of problematic experience, and in imagining more positive experience, multiple theoretical perspectives—interpretive, interactionist, critical, feminist, and postmodern—have been engaged. In this chapter I elaborate the focus on problematic experience and relations of power and emotion, state the assumptions guiding the study, present information regarding the specifics of data collection, and provide a critique of the current research on infant-toddler day care.

PROBLEMATIC EXPERIENCE, POWER, AND EMOTION

The set of activities examined herein are those minor epiphanic experiences for children in the care of adults who manage their daily activities and routines. *Problematic experience* is understood in contrast to the ready-to-hand or taken-for-granted realm of experience described by Heidegger (1927/1962), in which there are no ruptures in the flow of practical activity and experience.[2] Following Denzin (1989a) by epiphanic or problematic experience I refer to those moments in the lives of children and their caregivers which may (or may not) seem insignificant in themselves and their temporality, but which may be symbolically representative of major tensions, conflicts, or ruptures in their relationships, and which momentarily and cumulatively profoundly affect the meanings children give to themselves and their present and later experiences.

1

I focus particularly on problematic relations of power within the day care center. "Power is force or interpersonal dominance actualized in human relationships through manipulation and control" (Denzin, 1989a, p. 29); it is the imposition of one's will on the behavior of others, even against their will (Weber, 1962). Power is embedded in the microrelations of everyday life (Foucault, 1980), present in the daily routines and the emotional interactions between the children and their caregivers. Following Foucault, I study power not necessarily at the level of conscious intention or decision, but at the level of everyday practices, "where it installs itself and produces real effects" (1980, p. 97).

Emotion is integral to the relations of power and the experience of being powerful or powerless (Denzin, 1989a), and is therefore also a particular focus of the study. Moreover, children's emotional socialization is intricately tied to the emergence of their social selves (Gordon, 1985). Following Denzin (1984), emotions are understood as persons' self-feelings, experienced bodily, consciously, and in persons' social worlds.[3] Caregivers are significant emotional associates in children's lives, defining the "emotional culture" (Gordon, 1989a, 1989b) in and from which they develop their understandings about themselves, others, and their worlds.

The growing number of infants and toddlers in day care centers and the lack of research addressing their lived experiences point to the importance of this study. The most dramatic growth in the child day-care population has been among our youngest children—infants and toddlers, those children under three years of age.[4] More than half of all new mothers return to work before their children's first birthday (Child Care Action Campaign, 1988). One estimate is that more than five million infants and toddlers under the age of three have mothers working outside the home (Friedman, 1990). Most of these young children are cared for in family day care homes, but an increasing number are being enrolled in center-based group care programs (Hofferth & Phillips, 1987; Neugebauer, 1989).[5] It is the plight of these children that I address in this text.[6]

ASSUMPTIONS

This inquiry is situated within my personal experiences and convictions. In particular, two major assumptions guide my approach to this investigation. The first is that a primary goal of child rearing is to empower children by responding to their needs for attention and emotional security; by supporting their developing capacities to think, communicate, and act competently; and by providing opportunities for them to act autonomously, to make choices, and to be self-directed. The process of empowerment, I contend, begins in infancy.

While autonomy has long been a developmental goal in our culture (at least theoretically), we have constructed definitions of autonomy which emphasize self-reliance and separateness of self from others (Gilligan, 1988; Kagan, Kearsley, & Zelazo, 1980). My concern for autonomy does not preclude an equal concern for *connectedness*, or social and emotional intimacy. "A child's sense of self develops within a social context; autonomy grows out of attachment.... Autonomy and attachment have a figure-ground relationship—together they make up the gestalt of the complete adult" (Shanok, 1990, p. 3).

My second major assumption is that young children's daily experiences are as important as the outcomes of these experiences, thus the necessity of looking at their experience *as it is lived*. I am concerned that the necessary and legitimate attention to what we want children to *become* has taken disproportionate precedence over attention to who they are *now* and the *present quality* of their lived experience, the relationship of experience to future development and competencies notwithstanding.[7] In the words of Clarke-Stewart (1977), I am concerned that children have a "happy childhood . . . a time free from pressures and stress, a time for children to be themselves, find themselves, and express themselves" (p. 83). As Dewey (1900/1956) wrote,

> Life is the great thing after all; the life of the child at its time and in its measure no less than the life of the adult. Strange it would be indeed, if intelligent and serious attention to what the child *now* needs and is capable of in the way of a rich, valuable, and expanded life should somehow conflict with the needs and possibilities of later, adult life. (p. 60)

METHODOLOGICAL SPECIFICS

> We comprehend only part of what we see. . . .
> —Packer, *Interpretive Research and Social Development in Developmental Psychology*

My immersion into the worlds of the infants and toddlers I discuss here has consisted of five to ten hours a week over the past seven years observing in twelve infant and toddler class-rooms in six community licensed day care centers.[8] These centers represent a range of program types: church-based nonprofit, for-profit chains, corporate sponsored, and proprietary.[9] Four of these centers accept infants at six weeks of age, the other two between fifteen and twenty-four months. All are open for a ten- to twelve-hour day. All but one of these centers have a local, "word-of-mouth" reputation for being the "best." Both the university and the two-year community college place students in these centers for practicum experiences.

I observed in these programs as I supervised practicum students. In addition to my own observations, a considerable num-ber of field notes were recorded by practicum and independent study students enrolled in the university's child care training program. Observations occurred at various times in the day, from children's arrival through departure, in an attempt to get an overview of the entire day. Caregivers and students usually knew in advance when to expect me.[10]

My presence in these rooms ranged from minimal—unob-trusive observation—to participatory. The degree of my involve-ment varied with my assessment of the caregivers' comfortableness; I tried to be sensitive to caregivers' feelings and the demands of their work. Participatory involvement in these classrooms in-cluded having conversations with caregivers, talking and playing with the children, holding and comforting crying babies, inter-vening for safety reasons, and helping out in whatever ways I could when situations became hectic, as they often do in infant group care.

The field notes herein represent repeatedly observed situ-ations, within and across all these centers over the years, and pro-vide the foundation for my interpretations and understandings. By their presentation I invite the reader to see, hear, and experi-ence what my students and I have seen, heard and experienced. In the tradition of Coles (1967) and Polakow (1992), I often have drawn composite pictures, combining two or three similar inci-dents in order to emphasize and highlight the issues for the reader. I freely admit to the "poetizing" activity and evocative intent of interpretive phenomenological or ethnographic research (Clifford, 1986; Manen, 1984, 1990). In this process, I have attempted to be faithful to the words and gestures of those observed, at the same time noting that the writing of field notes is a corruption; something is "lost when a cultural world is textualized" (Clifford,

1986, p. 119). (See the Appendix regarding the credibility of interpretive accounts.)

Caregivers were aware of my research goals to varying degrees. My university supervisory role allowed for legitimate relations with these programs separate from any specific research purpose. I was there to observe my students, but the activities of the entire classroom were available to me as an integral part of those observations. I did, however, share my research goals with some programs (and parents) in some general terms, both written and verbal. But until the last few years I was unaware of my actual intentions and purposes beyond any general sense of wanting to understand children's daily experiences; my focus has been an emerging project.

RESEARCH ON
INFANT DAY CARE

The following commentary on the prevailing literature on infant day care is provided to contextualize the intent and purpose of this text. This review provides a background for the reader unfamiliar with the research literature and points to the need to address the issues I undertake in this project related to power and emotion in daily interactions.

Until recently, researchers who studied infant day care over the past twenty years generally concurred that "day care, when responsibly and conscientiously implemented, does not seem to have hidden psychological dangers" (Kagan, Kearsley, & Zelazo, 1980, pp. 261–62). The following excerpts provide some examples of the conclusions generally reached in these reviews.[11]

> In conclusion, research to date has revealed few significant differences between infants and toddlers cared for in group day care and those reared most exclusively by their mothers. (Kilmer, 1979, p. 112)

> With respect to emotional development, available evidence generally fails to support the notion that supplementary child care negatively affects the child. (Belsky, Steinberg, & Walker, 1982, p. 98)

Of central concern in most of these studies was the "effect" of substitute care on the mother-child relationship. Long-standing cultural attitudes advocating exclusive maternal child rearing have been reinforced by the literature of attachment theory (Ainsworth, 1964, 1970, 1973, 1979; Ainsworth, Blehar, Waters, & Wall, 1978; Bowlby, 1958, 1969, 1973). This theoretical perspective holds that attachment to a primary caregiver, the mother, is deemed essential for healthy psychological development in the early years, as well as children's later competence and social relationships. "An attachment is an affectional tie that one person forms to another person, binding them together in space and enduring over time" (Ainsworth, 1973, p. 1).

Attachment theory draws from ethology, evolutionary theory, pychoanalysis, and Piagetian developmental psychology, and was inspired by observations of institutionalized orphans who withered away and died in the absence of physical handling and loving attention (Karen, 1990). Built on studies of nonworking, middle-class mothers, attachment theory has influenced the focus of much of the infant day care research. While a full discussion of the merits of attachment theory are beyond the focus of this chapter,[12] some comments can be made here which are relevant to the approach to and limitations of the research on infant-toddler day care.

The primary question in most of this research has been the effect on attachment of a child's extended separation from his or her mother. In studying mother-child attachment researchers predominantly have employed the "Strange Situation," a twenty-one-minute laboratory procedure developed by Ainsworth which

> involves subjecting the young child to increasing levels of stress by repeatedly separating him or her from his or her mother and introducing him or her to a strange adult. The assumption underlying this experimental situation is that the child's approach-avoidance responses to mother and stranger, and willingness to explore the unfamiliar environment, index the quality of the infant-mother attachment bond. (Belsky, Steinberg, & Walker, 1982, p. 88)

Based on their performance, children are generally classified as securely or insecurely attached to their mothers, and the patterns revealed in this procedure are believed to be predictive of later social-emotional development. Display of anxiety in the young child is believed to reflect something amiss in the mother-infant bond (Kagan, 1979). This highly contrived laboratory procedure has dominated infant day care research—indeed, without the Strange Situation there would be hardly any research at all in this area. Use of the Strange Situation persists despite doubts expressed about its

> curious procedures involving mother, caretakers and strangers
> not only going in and out of rooms every minute for reasons quite
> obscure to the child but also not initiating interactions in the
> way they might usually do (Rutter, 1981, p. 160).

Not only is the assessment validity of these procedures questioned by some, but their predictive value, that is, the assumption that this early mother-child relationship determines later relationships, is also controversial (Kagan, 1984, 1987; Lewis, 1987). Questioning the theoretical assumptions of attachment theory, particularly those related to prediction versus description, Thompson (1987) pointed out that "a secure or insecure attachment in infancy, by itself, does not lead inevitably to certain psychosocial outcomes in children; it is the ongoing quality and consistency of care which is important" (p. 19; see also Thompson, 1988).

These issues notwithstanding, attachment theory continues to be the primary influence on infant day care research. And until recently, "the consensus among reviewers has been that day care does not unduly affect the child's attachment to the mother" (Belsky, 1988, p. 250). But in 1986 Jay Belsky challenged his own and others' previous conclusions with the publication of his article: "Infant Day Care: A Cause for Concern?" Belsky's early reviews of research on infant day care "found little if any evidence of detrimental effects of nonmaternal child care on infant development," especially in "model, university-based, research-oriented programs" (1986, p. 3) in which most of this early research was conducted. But upon reconsidering the evidence, Belsky (1986) reversed his earlier position, concluding that entry into care in the first year of life, for more than twenty hours a week, is a "risk factor"

> for the development of insecure-avoidant attachments in infancy
> and heightened aggressiveness, noncompliance, and withdrawal
> in the preschool and early school years. (p. 7)

Belsky's 1986 article sparked a debate among scholars and researchers which has taken place mainly in the journals *Zero to Three* (1987, 7 [3]) and the *Early Childhood Research Quarterly* (1988, 3 [3 & 4]), although it also has appeared in the popular press—magazines such as *Parents*, *The Atlantic*, *Newsweek*, and

Time (Galinsky & Phillips, 1988; Shell, 1988; Wallis, 1987; Wingert & Kantrowitz, 1990), as well as practitioner-oriented professional journals such as *Young Children* and the *Child Care Information Exchange* (Howes, 1989; Phillips, 1987a; see also Belsky, 1989). This debate has focused on whether infants in day care "at risk" for *later* social and emotional development.[13]

Belsky's critics for the most part take issue with his "selective" reading and interpretation of the available evidence. While not all question the validity of the Strange Situation, Belsky's critics question his interpretation of the meaning of children's behaviors in the Strange Situation. They suggest that children's personal histories and individual differences were overlooked, and that day-care children, used to daily separations and reunions, perceive the events in the lab differently, thus researchers ought not to interpret their Strange Situation behavior the same as for other (home-reared) infants. Critics also admonish Belsky for his premature conclusion, preferring to say "we still don't know" the effects of early day-care experience (Thompson, 1987, p. 20) and that the evidence is "complex and contradictory" warranting a "far more cautious and restricted conclusion" (Phillips, McCartney, Scarr, & Howes, 1987, pp. 19–20).[14]

In the following discussion, I raise three interrelated issues which have been minimally addressed in the infant day care controversy, and which point to the need for and intent of this project. These issues include the disproportionate focus on the mother-child relationship, the limited conception of emotional development, and the inadequate attention to the ongoing, daily experiences of infants and toddlers. All of these issues reflect the ideological nature of the day-care debate.

Focus on the Mother-Child Bond

Historical and contemporary attitudes toward women's roles have influenced not only the history and evolution of child care but the research focus of scholars caught in the ideological web of our society. Child care poses not only a challenge to our views about children, but what is suitable for women (McCartney & Phillips, 1988). Continuing a tradition that began with Locke, Rousseau, and Jefferson, and drawing support from psychoanalytic theory, attachment theory has made the mother the central experience and influence in a child's development, implicitly advocating a stay-at-home role for mothers (Karen, 1990). Research stressing the importance of the mother-child bond for all subsequent development drew upon observations of children in a particular historical period when only (primarily) mothers cared for children, thus leading to *normative* prescriptions that mothers are the most appropriate caregivers (Grubb & Lazerson, 1982). A repeated theme has been that babies require their mother's exclusive care (see, for example, White, 1981). Consider the following comments:

> No professional, however well-trained, will know a particular baby as well as a mother will know the infant she has cared for. And any professional, no matter how skillful, will be strange to a baby who from birth has been banking information ... emanating mostly from its mother. (Glickman & Springer, 1978, p. 113)

Consequently, the overwhelming concern in the day care research to date has been the effects of disrupting the mother-child bond, as mothers go to work outside the home. This is not a question asked when the father goes to work. While mothers are deemed essential to child rearing, a common belief is that "a good job can be done without a father in the home" (White & Watts, 1973, p. 242). Moreover, as Phillips (1987a) pointed out, concern for the mother-child relationship has seldom been an issue in all the years working-class women have held jobs, and upper-class women have traditionally hired help with child rearing, raising generations of children with the assistance of child caregivers. But as the number of middle-class working mothers has increased, who themselves were raised by at-home mothers, supplementary or substitute child care has become more of a public issue in the ideological debate over the role of women in our society.

McCartney and Phillips (1988) highlighted the ideological nature of the day care debate as it is tied to historical and societal conceptions of women, mothers, and families. They point out that, until recently, in our society, "any role for women other than motherhood has been portrayed as deviant" (p. 157). Consequently, "child care services are rarely portrayed as supportive and complementary to the family, unless accompanied by paternalistic motives to rectify the effects of deprivation" (p. 158) or maternal inadequacy.

The social and political ideology of motherhood is clearly reflected in the scientific literature in mother-child attachment theory and its huge role in child care research (McCartney &

Philips, 1988). Attachment theory asserts that children's emotional development depends on mothering. As a consequence, the study of child rearing has focused almost exclusively on the mother-child relationship; "shared childrearing [as in day care] is discussed within the context of *maladjustment*, for example, whether day care leads to attachment insecurity" (McCartney & Phillips, 1988, p. 164, italics added). Although attachment theorists may recognize that infants are capable of multiple attachments, research demonstrating and supporting this view is rarely done, revealing a consistent bias focused on the mother (Lewis, 1987).

    This overemphasis on the mother is clear in the overwhelming use of the Strange Situation, which has rarely engaged the participation of the father (and never in the evaluation of day care, to my knowledge). With few exceptions (e.g., Chase-Lansdale & Owen, 1987; L. Jones, 1985; Lamb, 1976) the father's emotional relationship with his child generally has been overlooked; "child care is never discussed in the context of paternal deprivation" (McCartney & Phillips, 1988, p. 158). The mother is, once again, held solely accountable for her child's development.[15]

    The specific interest in the developmental consequences of day care masks an ideological struggle, as rhetoric is couched in a language of concern for children but places this concern in a context that focuses on *maternal* responsibilities. The child care debate becomes a battleground that pits mothers against their children. Attachment theory and cultural values have shaped concerns in terms of the effects of more and more women working outside the home, as opposed to the nature and quality of children's experiences regardless of setting. For example, the literature repeatedly refers to the possible developmental outcomes of *maternal employment* (e.g., Benn, 1986; Hoffman, 1984; Lamb, 1982; Rubenstein, 1985; Weinraub, Jaeger, & Hoffman, 1988) or the "*detrimental* effects of *nonmaternal* child care" (Belsky, 1986, p. 63, italics added). This is almost always the phrasing, as opposed to a view that seeks to explore the quality of "extrafamilial" or "supplementary" group care, terms which suggest a different research focus. As Patricia Smith (1990) wrote, the phrase "working mother" demonstrates that the term "mother" is not a neutral descriptive term. The modifier "working" is indicative of the assumption that the term "mother" describes the norm of the married housewife who does not work outside the home for pay. We seldom hear the phrases "working father" or "paternal employment," especially expressed in terms of concern for children's development.[16] Thus the language reveals embedded assumptions and unstated norms that reflect and maintain attitudes about the status quo. In this way, the research rhetoric reveals an underlying ideology in the day care research that directs the political debate over day-care.[17]

Limited Conception
of Emotional Development

Insofar as infant day care research is grounded exclusively by attachment theory and the Strange Situation procedure, the conception and assessment of children's emotional development is extremely narrow. Emotions and emotional relationships are not static phenomena. "They cannot be taken out of context, classified, and quantified. They are processual . . . grounded in both time and place" (Power, 1986, p. 261).[18] As Kagan observed, the Strange Situation hardly reveals an emotional history between mother and child, and the overemphasis on (insecure) attachment ignores other aspects of parent-child relationships (quoted in Karen, 1990; see also Kagan, 1979). Also overlooked are the emotional relationships the child may have with other emotional associates (including other children), and the contributions of these relationships to emotional development (see Lewis, 1987). Specifically, the nature of the relationships the child in day care has, and what sort of emotional *experience* day care is, has been sorely neglected in research driven primarily by attachment theory (Calder, 1985, p. 252).

This is an ironic conclusion, given the revolutionary contributions of attachment theory to our understandings of infant emotional development. As Karen (1990) explained, attachment theory, blossoming in the heyday of behaviorism, was revolutionary in its contradiction of stimulus-response theory which asserted that picking up crying babies reinforced crying and dependent behavior. In contrast, attachment theory posits the critical importance of responsive care, both physical and emotional, from primary adults for children's developmental autonomy and competence. That is, a secure attachment is understood as the basis for growth, trust, and independence.

Attachment theory posits that the infant is social from the beginning, that all the infants' developmental processes are interlocked with personal interaction. Indeed, a child will not "thrive" without responsive interaction from a primary care figure. (Unfortunately, this figure is undoubtedly assumed to be the mother.) The child is perceived not as a passive recipient of care, or subject wholly to maturational or environmental processes, but as having an active role as he or she is encompassed in human relationships and engaged in symbolic interaction. The infants' socialization is a reciprocal process where both the adult and child make contributions to the relationship. Attachment theory stresses the importance of continuity of care, and the role of observation, interpretation, and empathy in understanding and responding to the infant. "Tracing the formation of attachment to care giving and responsiveness to relationships, Bowlby rendered the process of connection visible as a process of mutual engagement" (Gilligan, 1988, p. 10).

And so, it is not these premises of attachment theory with which I have difficulty. Indeed, to a great extent they underlie my interpretations of the field notes in this text. They parallel other theoretical perspectives (e.g., symbolic interactionism and interpretive phenomenology) in the importance given to the child's relations and experiences with others, and especially the importance attributed to the child's emotional life as inextricably linked to his or her development and socialization.

These contributions notwithstanding, attachment theory goes astray, I believe, first in its exclusive focus on the mother as the primary attachment figure and, second, in Ainsworth's attempt to quantify the study of this emotional relationship. While much of Ainsworth's early work involved "naturalistic" observation as she studied "real children in real environments," she contended that her twenty-one-minute Strange Situation procedure was more revealing than seventy-two hours of observation in children's homes (Karen, 1990, p. 47). With this move Ainsworth and her followers decontextualized the study of emotions and adult-child relationships, and contributed to a disproportionate emphasis (as with attachment theory overall) on the issue of mother-child separation in emotional development and the effects of day care.

Inadequate Attention
to Experience

A reading of the research reviews reveals an overwhelming quantitative orientation, not only in the use of the Strange Situation, but in the use of other procedures as well, and indicated by researchers' vocabularly: main effects, outcomes, time-sampling, frequencies, variables, statistical significance, mean scores, measures, correlates, and so on. Considerable emphasis is placed on outcome measures of children's development, as assessed by various standardized tests and (quasi-experimental) attachment studies.[19]

Both the quantitative orientation toward the "effects" on attachment and the ideological focus of the day care research contributes to the shockingly inadequate attention to children's ongoing experiences in day care programs. The focus is upon the effects of an infant's *separation* from his or her mother, rather than what happens to children *during* this separation. As Pawl (1990a) wrote, separation per se is only part of a far larger and perhaps more important issue—children's moment-to-moment experience:

> Understanding the experiences of infants in day care does not, as it sometimes seems to, primarily involve an understanding of issues of separation. In fact, that focus as the major issue of concern may be far more central to the experience of the parent than it is to the experience of the child. . . . Most vital . . . is that the infant or toddler is cared for in ways that promote his feeling effective, respected, and understood much of the time. If this occurs both with parents and with caregivers, then we have far less about which we must be concerned. (pp. 1–5)

The few studies that have attempted to focus on children's daily experiences and the quality of child care programs, while they may be "naturalistic," generally involve operationalizing, coding, and quantifying child and caregiver behaviors, which often result in an absence of content and contextualized understandings. For example, one study (Galluzzo, Matheson, Moore, & Howes, 1988) defined positive affect as smiling or laughing, and negative affect as expressing anger or protest. These simplified, decontextualized coding procedures overlook the idea that expressions of anger and protest can be regarded as *positive* developmental achievements in toddlerhood, indicative of separation and individuation, that is, growing independence and autonomy. In this way, research procedures often fail to provide contextualized understandings of the meanings of behavior for the children and caregivers in these settings.

Research articles and reviews typically close with reference to the incompleteness and inadequacy of research attempts to measure the effects of day care, methodological problems and constraints, sample and design limitations, and calls for better designed and controlled studies, more refined coding categories, elaborate ratings, and clinically sensitive measures.[20] At the same time concern is expressed for ecological validity![21] As Guttentag (1987) observed,

> noticeably absent from this discussion is any evaluation of the rearing conditions from the infant's or child's own *immediate* point of view. . . . To ignore completely the quality of experience from the infants' and children's perspectives is to deny the validity of their feelings. There should be more to evaluating the quality of child rearing than measuring its impact on later functioning. (p. 21, italics added)

SUMMARY

In this chapter I have stated the purpose of this project with regard to the focus on problematic relations of power and emotion in infant-toddler day care centers. I have described my guiding assumptions and the nature of data collection. I have reviewed the research in the field, noting the limitations which point to the importance of this work.

2
Theoretical and Philosophical Perspective

> How, then, do we come to understand the child's experiences? . . . [We] become anthropologists of childhood, recognizing that we are both embedded in, and yet distanced from, that very culture we once inhabited. . . . The hermeneutic task that such a commitment engenders engages the researcher in a quest for meaning and understanding. . . . It is the task of the adult "researcher" to uncover the existential ground of the everyday life experiences of the child and render them visible to those in power by giving them sensible actuality.
>
> —Polakow, *The Erosion of Childhood*

This study began as an open-ended inquiry. In the tradition of phenomenological investigation, my initial question was: "What is the nature of the lived experience for infants and toddlers in day-care centers?" And as children are not isolated apart from situations and others, the secondary question was: "What is the experience like for the children's caregivers?" More refined questions and understandings related to problematic experience, power, and emotion emerged as I continually returned to the phenomenon under investigation.

In this chapter I review the theoretical and philosophical framework informing my view of the child and of the research process, and my interpretations of problematic experiences related to power and emotion. The following perspectives are included: hermeneutic, existential phenomenology, symbolic interactionism, critical theory, postmodernism, and feminist theory. I conclude with a summary of the contributions of these diverse perspectives to this project.

It is important to note that the theoretical details and applications of these approaches vary according to the diversities among those who have developed and claimed them (Denzin, 1989a). This discussion is confined to aspects of these perspectives relevant to this particular study of children's lived experience; it is a positioning of myself in my work.[1] Further explanations of the historical development and contemporary divergences of these

15

traditions is beyond the scope of this project; the reader can pursue the sources cited throughout the text and notes.

HERMENEUTIC, EXISTENTIAL PHENOMENOLOGY

> Phenomenological research tries to understand the experiences of other people as they are constituted in actual everyday situations and to record the themes which may be found there. The goal is awareness, appreciation of the other's situation. . . . Where the child's world is of the utmost importance, phenomenological research can be used to make us aware of the experiences of the powerless and the powerful.
> —Barritt, Beekman, Bleeker, & Mulderij
> *A Handbook for Phenomenological Research in Education*

Phenomenology[2] is the task of describing what is given to us in immediate experience—our "life world" (Husserl, 1913/1962, 1970). It is through our experience, our "being-in-the-world" (Heidegger, 1927/1962, 1982) that we derive meanings. The understanding that lived experience is already meaningfully experienced is the basis of *hermeneutic phenomenology*, which combines the phenomenological task of description with the interpretation of meaning. Interpretation clarifies the meaning of experience and lays the groundwork for understanding (Denzin, 1989a). *Existential phenomenology* attends to action and praxis, dimensions of experience seen as fundamental to our being-in-the-world. Individuals are understood as conscious, intentional, active, choosing beings who constitute history and social process as they confront the everyday world with projects and choices. This view is extended to children in this project: "Children, when motivated by the practical problems of interacting with others, look back at, reflect on, and interpret what they have done" (Packer & Mergendollar, 1989, p. 71).

Interpretive perspectives[3] posit the fundamentally relational, social aspect of our existence and the inescapable fact that human beings are part of the world they study. Moreover, being-in-the-world is fundamental to knowing the world; everyday practices are the origin of our knowledge, they constitute who and what we are, and they structure our being-in-the-world (Packer, 1987). Far from being detached and neutral, interpretation begins from concerned engagement (Packer & Addison, 1989a, 1989b). Inquiry is inescapably value-bound; understanding is historically contingent and meanings are contextual. We cannot separate ourselves from interpretation. We see already understandingly and interpretively; there are always taken-for-granted assumptions or preliminary practical understandings. Interpretation and understanding are interwoven, are processual, develop over time, are bound up with language, and incorporate prior understandings. This is the "hermeneutic circle." The interpretive perspective acknowledges the incompleteness of our practical understandings and the unavoidable plurality of interpretations.

Interpretive studies, through ethnographic or "thick description,"[4] seek to reveal and disclose "the world as felt, lived, and experienced by those studied," to make meaningful and understandable their situated lived experience (Denzin, 1982, p. 22; 1989b). Recognizing that "social acts and events have meaning in a specific context or social setting" (Packer, 1987, p. 2), an interpretive approach allows the examination of child care as an ongoing process in the setting in which it occurs. Through description and interpretation the situated lived experiences of the children and their caregivers are made meaningful and understandable by bringing them before the reader (Denzin, 1989a). The researcher immerses herself into the everyday life-worlds of those studied—in this case, the child care center—and attends to the fundamental dimensions of these existential life-worlds: lived space, lived body, lived time, and lived human relations (Manen, 1990; see also Merleau-Ponty, 1962).

In this project I explore how these lived dimensions of time, space, body, and human relations are affected by the exercise of power and emotional estrangement. In particular, I draw upon Polakow's (1992) phenomenological study of child care and her discussion of temporal rigidity. In addition, my interpretations of children's problematic, epiphanic emotional experiences and the emotional culture of the day care setting are informed partly by a reading of Sartre's work on objectification, seriality, and alienation (1939/1962, 1943/1956, 1960/1963, 1960/1976).

SYMBOLIC
INTERACTIONISM

Human beings act toward things on the basis of the meanings that the things have for them.
—Blumer, *Symbolic Interactionism*

The interpretive position that human experience takes place in an elaborate network of social interaction is closely related to the significance attributed to social interaction and subjective interpretation by symbolic interactionism.[5] Symbolic interactionism is based on the beliefs that human behavior is self-directed, and that "human interaction is mediated by the use of symbols, by interpretation, or by ascertaining the meaning of one another's actions" (Blumer, 1969, p. 79).[6] In other words, interaction is mediated by an ongoing process of interpretation. Meanings emerge from interactions with others and influence interactions. The symbolic environment, then, is a shared environment (Shalin, 1986). Our self-perceptions, feelings, and actions tend to be mediated by how we perceive others see, feel, and act toward us.[7]

Childhood socialization, from the perspective of symbolic interactionism, is "a never-ending process that is negotiated and potentially problematic in every interactional episode . . ." (Denzin, 1977, p. 3).[8] Infants are immediately drawn into the social world. They enter the world of symbolic behavior through experience and association with others. The newborn's slightest expressions elicit responses from parents, siblings, and strangers— they become partners in the give and take of human relationships (Snow, 1989). Relationships, formed and grounded in interactive episodes, are the nexus of socialization. The child's self arises in the fluid interplay between and among people in social situations, mediated by language. It is this conversation of symbolic gestures that links children with their caregivers. Although nonverbal, infants are expressive and communicative interactants, social and emotional beings within social situations. While children are active participants in their socialization process, the meanings they assign to their own and others' gestures are largely dependent on the meanings given to them by their caregivers in their responses and gestures. In other words, to a great extent, children come to see and feel about themselves as they perceive their primary caregivers to feel about them.

In common with interpretive researchers, the symbolic interactionist studies "group life and conduct" in the setting in which it occurs (Blumer, 1969, p. 47), and is concerned with the relationships between how we see ourselves, how we see others, and how we think others see us (Manen, 1990). This project, informed by a reading of Goffman (1959, 1961, 1967), looks at power partly from an interactionist perspective, particularly as I describe the ways in which the caregivers define how the children will be regarded, understood, and treated (see Becker, 1973).

The interactionist perspective also informs my view of emotion (see Denzin, 1984, 1985; Gordon, 1981, 1989a, 1989b; Power, 1985a, 1985b, 1986; Shott, 1979). For the symbolic interactionist, emotions are "emerging acts under construction and definition by the individual" (Gordon, 1985, p. 141), "grounded in the practical activities that locate individuals in the world" (Denzin, 1984, p. 32). Children's emotional socialization is intricately tied to the emergence of their social selves. In recurring emotional episodes, children learn from their caregivers what is acceptable and unacceptable behavior; they learn what Hochschild (1979, 1983) calls "feelings rules" and how to do "emotion work." The interactionist perspective is specifically apparent in the applications of Hochschild's (1979, 1983) work on emotional labor to the interpretation of the emotional culture of the day-care setting.

CRITICAL THEORY

There is no such thing as a *neutral* educational process.
—Shaull, Introduction in Freire's *Pedagogy of the Oppressed*

I turn to critical theory in my concern for children's empowerment, their freedom to construct meanings and situations— to "name their world" (Freire, 1970, p. 76). Critical theorists look at forms of social control, how time and space organize and monitor the body, and how social identities are produced by institutionalized power (McLaren, 1989). The "powerful facticity of the social situation" is a fundamental premise of critical theorists (Rabinow & Sullivan, 1979, p. 15). In common with interpretive and interactionist perspectives, critical theory posits that persons are active agents in the construction of their personal lives and social worlds (Comstock, 1982); "the individual both creates and is created by the social universe of which he/she is a part" (McLaren, 1989, p. 166).[9] The contradictions of this dialectic are a particular focus of critical theorists.

Critical research projects begin with the subjects' lifeworlds, their life problems, and intersubjective understandings. This project is "critical" as I explore the hegemony produced in the everyday routines and rituals of the day care center (Giroux, 1981). I examine how children and their caregivers are enculturated and subjected to oppressive practices and ideologies, and look for places of resistance.

Grounded in a concern for understanding and emancipatory praxis, critical pedogogical thought is reflected in the works of Freire (1970, 1985), Giroux (1981, 1991a, 1991b), and McLaren (1986, 1989, 1991), among others, but tends to focus on older children and adults. These students are considered to be competent dialogic participants, able to participate in the unmasking of the hegemony they experience. An unaddressed issue in the crtical theory literature is at what point and in what ways young children are able to engage in "dialogue," "conversation," or to "name their world," and to what extent adults ought to do the "naming" for children in the interests of acculturation, socialization, and education. Given developmental differences, it is not clear to what extent a critical approach can be applied to very young children in day care. A central question that emerges in the interpretation of their experience, however, is how caregivers enter into the lives of children, give children "voice," and allow them to "name their world." This project is, in part, an extension of the critical pedagogical project, as the experience of infancy, early childhood, and early institutional care has been virtually left out of this discourse, with the notable exception of Polakow (1992).

Confronting participants of a study with the researcher's understandings is fundamental to interpretive, critical projects (Denzin, 1989a; Comstock, 1982). Caregivers' own voices, their thoughts, and their words on behalf of themselves are largely absent from this text; hence here I am remiss in the critical project to enter into a dialogue engaging caregivers in their own self-understandings (and the postmodern project to legitimate local, personal understandings). I explain this limitation further in chapter 6 and I am addressing this ommission in current work (see Leavitt, 1993a, 1993b).

FEMINISM

> The methods and outcomes of science and its ideal of control
> are far from neutral and indifferent to gender.
> —Hein, "The Feminist Challenge to Science"

This project also draws support and inspiration from feminist theory. In common with interpretive perspectives, considerable feminist theory asserts the importance of lived experience as providing the grounding for our understandings, and seeks to understand the meanings persons give to their actions and situations.[10] The feminist task is an interpretive phenomenological task insofar as feminists attend to and incorporate personal experience in the attempt to make persons' lives intelligible.[11] In this process feeling, subjectivity, intimacy, and love are not regarded as inadequate when juxtaposed to male-scientific virtues of reason, objectivity, autonomy, and power—rather, they are regarded as enriching feminist inquiry.

The historical and political construction of women and gender relations is at the center of feminist philosophy.[12] Questions are posed in the context of a contemporary society perceived as patriarchal. Relations of power in contemporary society, specifically as these are gender-based, is a central issue. How these relations are manifested in and are realized, and how they influence, control, and shape persons' everyday lived experience, particularly as these experiences are problematic for women, is the focus of much feminist theory (see D. E. Smith, 1979, 1987).

Feminist theory attempts to go beyond explanation and understanding, emphasizing the empowerment of women and the development of (specifically feminist) alternatives. Based on the conviction that persons can intervene and provoke social change, feminist philosophy is seen as a transformative activity (Gatens, 1986). Understanding and empowerment are both achieved primarily through "consciousness-raising," or critical reflection on individuals' ongoing lived experience, particularly as this experience has been made problematic by existing gender relations.[13]

I draw from feminist theory as I turn my attention toward the female caregiver and the problematics with which she is confronted as she is caught in the flow of daily interactions. It is primarily feminists who call attention to the problematic situation of the caregiver. A feminist perspective also has been applied to the deconstruction of the prevailing literature on infant-toddler day care (chapter 1), particularly in its focus on the mother-child bond.

In my constructions and interpretations of the meanings of care and caring within day-care centers, I draw support from recent feminist philosophy stressing the social and emotional interdependence all human beings. This body of feminist thought stresses the importance throughout life, for both sexes, of "being-in-relation," the connection between ourselves and others, and the essential role of caring to our welfare (Gilligan, 1982, 1988; Gilligan & Wiggins, 1988; Grimshaw, 1986). Feminist essays on mothering and care (e.g., Noddings, 1984, 1992; Diller, 1988; Ruddick, 1983, 1987, 1989) point to the importance of intersubjectivity, emotionality, empathy, particularity, and entering the world of the other in conceptualizing caring relationships.[14] In this view, autonomy and empowerment are not contrary to, but dependent upon, relationships and maintaining connectedness with specific contexts.

POSTMODERNISM

> Whatever we write conveys meanings we do not or could not possibly intend, and our words cannot say what we mean.
> —Harvey, *The Condition of Postmodernity*

Postmodernism is an elusive term to define, representing a blurring of boundaries in academic disciplines (Featherstone, 1988; Harvey, 1989; Kellner, 1991).[15] It refers both to a historical period since World War II—a time of a crisis in faith and of legitimation, personal and public confusion, and an eclectic mix of theoretical discourse, many in tension with each other (Denzin, 1986a; Giroux, 1991a; Mills, 1959).[16] A number of writers have discussed the affinity between postmodernism and feminism (e.g., Diamond & Quinby, 1988; Flax, 1987; Fraser & Nicholson, 1988; Morris, 1988; Nicholson, 1989; Owens, 1983; Sawicki, 1988). Likewise, the intersections of hermeneutics and postmodernism have been noted (Caputo, 1987; Madison, 1990), and others attempt to bridge postmodernism and critical theory (Giroux, 1991a, 1991b; Kellner, 1991; Lather, 1991; McLaren, 1986, 1991), theoretical contradictions notwithstanding.

This project is "postmodern" in the absence or abandonment of the quest for certainty; fundamental knowledge; transcendental, objective, ahistorical, and absolute truth; and universal consensus. From the postmodern standpoint, there are no fixed or value-free facts. Science is seen as just "one particular way in which humans tell stories and refigure the world of lived experience" (Madison, 1990, p. 46). The accounts presented here are "stories," fictions insofar as they are my constructions and representations of the experiences of others and myself, and my interpretations of these experiences (see Clifford, 1986; Denzin, 1989b, 1990). My intent is to provide telling interpretations that focus attention and offer insight, not to capture meaning absolutely.

The postmodern project challenges our taken-for-granted understandings and embraces the problematic and a bringing forth of controversies. In the spirit of postmodern inquiry, I note the increasing complexity and contradictions of the understandings presented here and do not pretend an increasing clarity and closure (Hoy, 1988). The eclectic selection of texts applied herein reflects the postmodern contention that disciplinary boundaries are blurred. I adopt the postmodern position that no one interpretation is the authoritative truth; no one method is the method for understanding. To "write postmodern" (Lather, 1991) is to avoid totalizing, fixed meanings.[17] My descriptions of children and their caregivers, as postmodern ethnographies, are fragmentary (Tyler, 1986). There is considerable experience, thought, and emotion that exists beyond this "narrative capture" and which cannot be represented directly (Denzin, 1990).

The contemporary experience of children in day care has been described as a postmodern childhood (Denzin, 1987b; Leavitt & Power, 1989). The postmodern "self is constructed as a terrain of conflict and struggle" (Giroux, 1991a, p. 30). As a postmodern interpretation of children's experience, this study illuminates the problematic construction of children's development and their understandings of themselves, others, and their world. This postmodern ethnography illuminates children's developmental, situated "otherness," and their status as a marginalized group.

In particular, this postmodern interpretation of problematic relations of power between the children and their caregivers is informed by a reading of Foucault (1975/1979a, 1980). I apply Foucault aware that he was distrustful of themes of liberation and the idea of a foundational self that is repressed and alienated (Foucault, 1984/1988). As Fraser (1989) noted, "there is no foundation, in Foucault's view, for critique oriented around the notions of autonomy, reciprocity, mutual recognition, dignity, and human rights" (p. 56). Yet Foucault's emphases on developing accounts of how persons are constituted through power relations, the microrelations of power, and his thesis that "power is exercised rather than possessed" (Foucault, 1975/1979a, p. 26), inspired and informed the interpretation of the field notes herein.

Postmodern discourse, with its stress on contingent or absent meanings and continual deconstruction, has been criticized for leaving us in a relativistic void, with no vision of a better society, no place for the human subject, and no way to claim values or meaningfully address viable social change and reasoned action. At the same time the authenticity of marginalized voices is acknowledged, they are shut off from access to empowering discourses (Harvey, 1989); human agency is obscured or even denied (Colapietro, 1990). These issues suggest that a postmodern standpoint, alone, provides inadequate guidance in developing grounded understandings of children's experiences or in answering the question: How do we care for our children?

It is at this point I turn away from postmodern discourse and return to the traditions of interpretive, interactionist, critical, and feminist theory. Such a move enables me to address issues of autonomy, empowerment, and reciprocity—primarily modernist concerns.[18] It is the modernist who believes in human promise and potential, renewal and change, and who is hopeful in engaging the contradictions of our times (Berman, 1988). Thus, some of the assumptions and concerns underlying this thesis may be modernist, but I take, at times, a postmodern approach in addressing them.

Interpretive perspectives allow a view of the human subject as a self-reflective, interpreting, active, and interactive meaning-maker, although constructed and constrained within social, historical, political, and economic situations, a subject capable of developing critical understandings of these situations and *changing* them. Interpretive, interactionist, critical, and feminist perspectives, in their emphases on self-directed actors, enlightenment, and empowerment, offer both a "language of critique and possibility" (Giroux, 1991a).[19] What Giroux (1991b) characterizes as a "postmodernism of resistance" (p. 232) posits a faith in social transformation, and points to solidarity, community, and compassion as essential to developing meaningful understandings of ourselves and our joint experience in the world.

SUMMARY

> All topics are available—all its applications are legitimate, all methods are feasible; all interdisciplinary connections are accessible.
> —Castañeda, "Philosophy as a science and as a world view" in Cohen & Dascal, *The Institution of Philosophy*

In this chapter I have reviewed the theoretical and philosophical framework informing this study. The value of these diverse discourses lies in their contributions and challenges to our understandings of ourselves, others, and our social world—and the research process. Their contributions amount to a view of children and their caregivers as meaning-makers engaged in joint acts, potentially problematic, and constructed and constrained by the specific and at-large social situations in which they find themselves. Interpretive, interactionist, critical, feminist, and postmodern discourses all posit the value-bound context of our observations and interpretations. Interpretations and understandings of situated, ongoing, everyday life experiences of particular individuals, specifically as these experiences are problematic, are developed within the immediate contexts in which they occur. The understandings which emerge are viewed as social constructions, value-laden, historically specific, grounded in experience, and always incomplete.

This pluralistic approach toward understanding children's lived experience should not be perceived as a totalizing one which attempts a final, integrated, cohesive theoretical approach. The pluralistic approach reflects instead the postmodern rejection of metatheory and the presumption of a single method.[20] It is a pragmatic call to tailor methods to fit the specific problems and situations I want to understand, and it is a recognition of the diversity and contradictions of continually emerging understandings.

Heretofore, these perspectives have focused primarily on *adult* life. Developmental and situational differences between adults and children notwithstanding, "children engage in behavior that is every bit as humanly social as the sequences of actions routinely undertaken by . . . adults" (Denzin, 1977, p. 93). The child, too, is a meaning-maker as she participates in the world and assigns meaning to experience. Thus, the undertaking of this multi-theoretical approach to a study of children's lived experience in day care centers is also an exploration of their applicability in developing understandings of the life-worlds where adults and children are placed together.

This multitheoretical interpretive approach makes possible the vivid description and moving interpretation of children's lived experience. It allows me to make sense, however transitory and incomplete, of children's life-worlds, in the endeavor to create a more responsive and empowering world for children and their caregivers. Philosophical description and understanding is then, hopefully, praxis.

> The aim, once again then, is to approach, then describe what there is that seems to matter. (Coles, 1967, p. 41)

3
Power

Time penetrates the body and with it all the meticulous controls of power.
                    —Foucault, *Discipline and Punish*

In this chapter I explicitly address problematic relations of power between the children and their caregivers, and present illustrative field notes. I begin with a description of the day care setting as an institution that imposes a temporal and spacial regime on the lives of infants and toddlers. As Harvey (1989) wrote, "spatial and temporal practices are never neutral in social affairs" (p. 239). Drawing primarily from Goffman, Foucault, and Polakow/Suransky, I illustrate how the caregivers' command over children's bodies in space and time is a fundamental, pervasive source of social power in and over the children's everyday lives. Field notes illustrate how caregivers create problematic situations for the children as they exercise their power in the rigid management of daily routines, and the ways in which caregivers control and contain children's play. I also describe how children's efforts to resist the caregivers' power are often undermined. I contrast the illustration of the caregivers' extractive power with a discussion of developmental, transformative power. I close the chapter with further reflections on these experiences as indicative of children's place in the world of day care.

SPATIAL REGIME

Space is fundamental in any exercise of power.
                    —Foucault, *The Foucault Reader*

In these day care centers, two or three caregivers share responsibility for about eight to as many as sixteen infants and/or toddlers each day. Infants and toddlers are grouped into classrooms according to state licensing standards which mandate adult-child ratios and maximum group size enrollments by age and set minimum square footage requirements accordingly, about thirty-five to fifty-five square feet of space per child, depending upon whether sleep and play space are combined. The newer buildings usually have direct exits from the classroom to outdoor play space, but programs housed in churches often do not have easy access—for example, the largest program I visited housed the infants up one flight of stairs and had no playground. Caregivers in this center sometimes took the children to a nearby park, but the youngest infants generally were confined to one room throughout the day (as were the caregivers, but who, as employees, had scheduled short breaks when they could leave the room).

Some of these rooms were decorated quite cheerfully, with bright colors and pictures on the walls—the surface appearance is that they are happy places to be. Other rooms, generally in the church-based older programs, looked more "school-like" and even bare. In general, while some rooms had shelves of assorted toys, there was often a utilitarian aspect to the space. The arrangement of the rooms was determined by the necessity of custodial routines: cribs and high chairs bordered the walls or took up the room in rows, dominating infant rooms; toddler rooms had tables for eating and artwork, and cots stacked up until nap time.

For a major portion of their day (up to ten hours or more) all the aspects of children's lives—sleeping, playing, and eating—are conducted in one place and according to the shared authority of the caregivers. This is the children's lived and felt space. The confinement to and arrangement of the physical environment provides the condition of "enclosure," a space "closed in upon itself" (Foucault, 1975/1979a, p. 141), and allows for the exercise of power first by containment and surveillance.

The two toddler rooms are divided by a movable partition, which is open in the mornings as the children arrive. After the morning snack, the younger toddlers are to stay on their half of the room. Today Gordie decided to walk over to the other side of the room. The student began to approach him, to explain why he had to return to his side of the room. Before she reached him, the caregiver loudly called from across the room "Gordon Grant, NOW!" Gordie, startled and intimidated, returned to the proper side of the room.

In these situations children's mobility is contained and confined within certain demarcated boundaries. Space is not an *extension* into which children may flow and extend themselves, rather, space is experienced as a *restriction* (Suransky, 1977, p. 299).

*Every morning and afternoon the toddlers play in the base-
ment gym. The adults sit on chairs lined up on one side of the room
and watch the children. The children are told these are "teachers'
chairs" and they are not allowed to sit on them. There are no "child
chairs." Today, Jill climbed up on an empty chair and was told to get
off. "Who are these chairs for?" the adult asked Jill. "Teachers," she
replied. "OK, now go play," directed the caregiver.*

The organization of the day care space allows for the practice of discipline while at the same time discipline organizes the
space (Foucault, 1975/1979a). This is illustrated in the situations below, as caregivers controlled children's activities by the
arrangement of the room and the materials made available to
the children.

*The toy shelves in the toddler room reach a height of about
four-and-a-half feet from the floor. Children are allowed to choose
from a sparse number of toys on the lower shelves, but toys on the
top shelves are made available only at the caregivers' discretion. The
caregiver told the student she didn't want "too many" toys out.*

*Toya (six months) likes to play with the "busy boxes" tied to
the side of the infant cribs. But when she attempted to play with them
at nap time, the caregiver said "NO!" because, explained the caregiver, "she should be sleeping." When Toya woke up from her nap,
she was also prohibited from this play, because "she must stay on
the carpet with the other babies." The caregivers did not bring the
busy box to the carpet for Toya.*

*The only toys on the shelves in this room are some books,
and a few Fisher-Price materials. The selection is the same everyday. There is a housekeeping corner, but children are allowed to play
there only with the adult's permission. As a special treat every day
the caregivers introduce one new toy from the storage area, such as
"bristle blocks" or dress-up clothes, which the entire group must
share or take turns. They are able to play with these materials, while
supervised, for a limited amount of time. The children are made to
keep the toys in one area of the room. I asked the caregiver why ma-
nipulatives and other toys were not available everyday. She replied
that they were only for special occasions.*

Beyond containment and surveillance, power was more
explicitly exercised in the management of children's activities and

routines within these settings, what Foucault (1975/1979a) described as "disciplinary time" (p. 151).[1]

DISCIPLINARY TIME

> Time is not a line but a network of intentionalities.
> —Merleau-Ponty, *The Phenomenology of Perception*

Children's daily routines in the day-care center are tightly scheduled, with one activity leading at a prearranged time into the next, the whole sequence of activities being imposed from above by a system of formal rulings. Foucault (1975/1979a) described this as the organization of "serial space" (p. 147). Infant schedules are typically organized according to "custodial" routines: eating, sleeping, and diaper changing. Infants may "play" or sit in infant swings or seats between these routines. As children get older (about fifteen months) more is added to the schedule, typically adult-directed activities, such as story time, art, or music. A schedule, or "time-table" (Foucault, 1975/1979a, p. 149), is often posted on the wall, as was this one:

Toddler Daily Schedule

7:30–8:30	Arrival/Free play in the room
8:30–8:50	Group time
	(calendar, story, fingerplays)
8:50–9:20	Breakfast
9:20–9:30	Cleanup/Toileting
9:30–10:30	Teacher-directed activity
	(e.g., "art," music, etc.)
10:30–11:00	Outdoors or gym
11:00–11:20	Free play
11:20–11:30	Washing and toileting
11:30–12:00	Lunch
12:00–2:30	Nap time
2:30–3:00	Toileting
3:00–3:15	Snack
3:15–3:30	Group time
3:30–4:00	Teacher-directed activity
4:00–4:30	Outdoors or gym
4:40–5:00	Toileting
5:00–5:30	Free play

These daily activities are carried on within a shared group setting; children are always in the company of other children, all of whom are treated alike and are required to do the same thing together. Goffman (1961) described this as "collective regimentation" (p. 6). As the schedule indicates, children, as a group, are often required to go through fifteen or more transitions, or change of activity, each day. The schedule serves to tell the day care staff what they will be doing at any given moment and implies that children, left on their own, could not initiate and organize their own actions (Denzin, 1973b). Moreover,

> the seriation of successive activities makes possible a whole investment of duration by power: the possibility of a detailed control and a regular intervention . . . in each moment of time. . . . Power is articulated directly onto time; it assures its control and guarantees its use. (Foucault, 1975/1979a, p. 160)

The relationship between time and power is described in the field notes below, as schedules dictate children's experiences.

Many of the toddlers had already eaten when they arrived this morning, yet breakfast was served immediately. All the children were required to sit at the table.

The children appeared sleepy about a half hour before lunchtime, at least an hour still to go before the scheduled nap time, yet they were forced to stay awake through the lunch period.

The caregiver insisted that all the infants have an afternoon nap. Kim (six months) had only a one-half hour nap early this afternoon, but was sitting contentedly on the carpet surrounded by toys. Without any visible indication that she was sleepy or fussy, the caregivers decided Kim should take a nap. Kim's play was interrupted and she was put in her crib; she lay there quietly with her eyes wide open, sucking on a blanket. When she started whimpering about thirty minutes later, I moved to pick her up out of her crib, but was told by the caregiver, "No, she'll go to sleep eventually." Kim started crying and screaming ten minutes later. I moved again to pick her up and was told to leave Kim, that she'd go to sleep eventually. After twenty more minutes of her crying, one of the caregivers picked her up and gave her a bottle and then Kim stayed up the rest of the afternoon. Kim was in her crib for one hour total—without closing her eyes once.

As Goffman noted in his description of total institutions, the organization and management of daily routines reflect an underlying rationale—the securement of children's compliance for an orderly day and the supposed benefits to their development. Consider the following field notes.

> When the toddlers were done eating their lunch, they were to stay seated until called to wash their hands and brush their teeth. They were called in the order they finished eating. Several children finished eating about the same time, so some of them waited a long time to be called, doing nothing but sitting. When a child got out of his chair, he had to go back and sit down for a little while before being called. Carrie, on her own initiative, got out of her seat and waited by the sink. When the caregiver refused to let her wash her hands and brush her teeth, Carrie began to cry; it was clear that she was quite upset. The caregiver told Carrie she needed to sit down until she was called. Neither caregiver tried to comfort her or help her back to her seat. After about five minutes of crying, the caregiver irritatedly told Carrie to go lie down on her cot, without washing or brushing.

In this situation, the concept of allowing children to initiate and carry out their own handwashing was subordinate to the adult's prearranged schedule and implementation procedures.

> Before the children (two-year-olds) were permitted to sit at the table and eat their lunches, the caregiver had them identify their names, written on large name tags she had made. All the children sat on the rug while the caregiver randomly selected and held up a name tag directly in front of the child whose name it was. That child then was to identify him or herself by saying his or her name and then was permitted to sit down at one of the tables (and wait again for lunch to be served). The other children had to remain sitting on the carpet and wait for their name tags to be shown. They were told to sit on their "bottoms." If they stood, or began to walk over to the tables on their own initiative, they were told to sit down; their names were then called last. Today the caregiver mistakenly held out the wrong name tag in front of one little boy. He called out his own name and jumped up to sit down at the table. Another little girl said "me" when the caregiver held out her name tag.

The above field notes suggest that (at least some) children may not be "reading" their names, but have merely learned the procedure. But some of the necessary dispositions for participation in this culture, that is, waiting, turn-taking, and compliance, are secured. Thus, caregivers' adherence to, and implementation of, the schedule stipulates normative standards for the children's behavior. The field notes below illustrate again the nature of the caregivers' power over children, as they are made to conform to the norms stipulated by the schedule.

During lunchtime the toddlers were tired. Today Jules (sixteen months) started to fall asleep at the table. He was roused and encouraged to eat, as the adult said, "it's not time to sleep yet." When this was not enough to wake Jules, the caregiver jostled his chair in an attempt to awaken him. When that didn't work, Jules was removed from the chair and stood up in another attempt to keep him awake. Only after the lunch period was over was Jules cleaned up and permitted to nap on his cot.One day, Jules was falling asleep the minute he sat down for lunch. The caregiver tried to get him to stay awake and to eat, but he responded by crying. After only a minute of crying, he started to fall asleep again, food in his mouth. At this point, one of the caregivers tried to get him to stand up, but his legs just folded underneath him. She sat him back on his chair, and turned her attention to another child. Before anyone had time to prevent it, Jules fell out of his chair. He was definitely awake then!

It was snack time and all the children were directed to stop playing and sit at the table. Maggie (fourteen months) pushed her food away and began to cry. The caregiver said perhaps Maggie was tired and removed her from the table to change her diaper and then sat down to hold and rock her. Maggie squirmed in her arms, refusing to sit still. The caregiver let her down on the floor where she played contentedly. Observing this, the caregiver said to the other adults, "Next time Maggie must sit through snack time. She wasn't tired, she just wanted to play."

The caregiver in the last situation above initially appeared to demonstrate some flexibility, excusing and attempting to comfort a child she perceived to be too tired to eat a snack. When she discovered that Maggie just "wanted to play," however, she asserted that this was not a justifiable reason to be excused from the snack table. The child's inclinations were subordinate to a higher ruling.

In the field notes thus far, the schedules appear to be arbitrarily planned and implemented, in the absence of any observation and interpretation of the children's experiences. Scheduled routines were given primacy over the children's inclinations; their understandings and expressions of their own feelings of fatigue, hunger, and energy were denied, and subordinated to adult-imposed schedules. Polakow (1992) described this as the imposition of "temporal rigidity" (p. 61). As infants are subjected to this discipline and rigidity, their lived-time world is refashioned into the metacategories of institutional time (Polakow, 1992). By enforcing the schedule above all else, and rigidly managing transitions, caregivers exercise their control and power. As the children's "time controllers" (Polakow, 1992, p. 65), they make children do what they wouldn't otherwise—sleep, eat, line up, be silent, sit, wait, be still. In Foucault's (1975/1979a) terms, the effect of the caregivers' discipline is to produce "docile bodies" (p. 138).

If a toddler doesn't go to bed "cooperatively," the caregiver will put him or her on the cot, face down, and put one arm across the back of the child's neck, and the other arm over the child's ankles, holding the child down. The caregiver remains in that position until the child falls asleep. No reasons are given to the children for why this is done. They are simply told they have to stay on their cots.

The caregiver set up a table with glue and cotton balls and precut paper squirrels, each with a child's name already written on it. She sat down and called the toddlers, who had been sitting in a group on the carpet waiting, over one at a time. Only one child at a time could do the activity; the others were to wait with the group, supervised by another caregiver leading "fingerplays." Children who were not sitting still were called to the table last. "I won't call you until you sit down!" the caregiver said to Shana, who had started to move over to the table on her own. She looked at the caregiver and sat down, and waited expectantly for her name to be called, not attending to the fingerplays. The caregiver called another child over, while Shana watched. When a turn opened up, the first caregiver turned to the second and asked if she should call "her." The caregiver, engaged in her fingerplays, glanced up and replied, "no." Two more children had their turns, and then Shana was called over.

It was "group time" before the morning snack. The caregiver was leading all ten toddlers in a movement activity. The songs and dances were complex and the children were not paying attention. The second caregiver announced that the snack was ready, at which point the first caregiver stopped in the middle of a song, directed the children to sit down, and began calling the children's names one by one to tell them they could move to the tables and sit down for snack. Eventually she turned to Nathan and said, "Well, Nathan isn't sitting on his carpet square, so I can't call him to the table." She went on calling the names of other children who were seated. After all the other toddlers had been called, the caregiver said, "Nathan still isn't sitting on his carpet square. Nathan, I can't call you unless you're sitting down." Nathan did not move; he seemed distracted by the activity at the snack tables. The caregiver went over to him and physically manipulated him into a sitting position onto a carpet square. She then said, "Nathan, you can go sit at the table, now." Nathan complied.

The above episodes illustrate how discipline requires both the correct use of time and the correct use of the body (Foucault, 1975/1979a), as the child's body is manipulated according to the caregivers' authority. The rule that a child must be sitting before he can be allowed to move to another activity seems arbitrary, to exist for no other purpose than to give the caregiver a feeling of control over the children and the management of daily routines. It is doubtful that the toddlers understood why they must sit on the carpet squares, but the use of physical force does suggest to them that they must comply with the caregiver's directions or they will be made to. I asked this last caregiver if she thought Nathan understood what he was being asked and she replied, "I don't know, but he'll learn sometime."

Disciplinary norms are also communicated to children in more subtle, less physical ways. The following episode may appear unproblematic in itself but implies a normative standard for the children to follow.

The caregiver entered the darkened classroom at 2:30. The infants were just awakening from their naps; some were still asleep. The caregiver announced to the room in general, "You guys are so good!" She turned to me to explain, "They usually wake up at 1:00."

In this situation the children were considered "good" because they stayed asleep until the end of the *scheduled* nap time, a physiological state of being not under their control. In this way children construct understandings about their behavior and themselves through caregiver practices. "In discipline, punishment is only one element of a double system: gratification-punishment. And it is this system that operates in the process of training and correction" (Foucault, 1975/1979a, p. 180).

CAREGIVER POWER/
CHILDREN'S PLAY

> Play is not only the child's response to life; it is his life if he is
> to be a vital, growing, creative individual.
> —(Hartley & Goldenson, *The complete book of children's play*

Thus far, the field notes presented illustrate how caregivers create or exacerbate problematic situations for the children as they exercise their power in the rigid management and implementation of daily (largely custodial) routines and transitions. The power exerted by caregivers is also evident in the ways in which they control and contain children's play.

The lack of flexibility that would have allowed Toya (p. 00) to play with the busy boxes on the floor or in her crib until she fell asleep is demonstrated again, this time in two different toddler rooms.

Cyril (twenty months) chose a shape sorter toy to play with— a spherical plastic ball with holes cut out to match shapes placed inside it. Cyril decided to use the toy as a bowling ball. The caregiver immediately yelled at him, "This is not a ball!" and redirected his use of the toy.

The caregiver took out some playdough for the children. As children approached her at the table she gave each some dough (they weren't allowed to help themselves). The caregiver demonstrated how to scrunch, roll, and shape the dough. Karen (seventeen months) approached the table and was given some dough. She poked at it for a few minutes and then began to walk away from the table. The caregiver stopped her and asked, "Karen, are you done?" Karen looked at her and replied, "done." The caregiver asked if she was sure and again Karen said "done." The caregiver washed Karen's hands and Karen went elsewhere to play. A few minutes later Karen walked back to the table and picked up some dough. The caregiver said, "Karen, you're done playing with the dough. You left the table and said you were finished, so go find something else to play with." Karen tentatively touched the dough again and the caregiver repeated, "No, Karen, you're done." Karen turned around and left with a disappointed and confused expression. A few minutes later she returned to the table and watched the other children. The practicum student then distracted Karen by suggesting they play together in the housekeeping corner.

In both these situations the caregivers restricted the children's initiative, intentionality, and sense of control over their own activity. The word "done" had different meanings for Karen and her caregiver, just as Cyril and his caregiver had different ideas of "ball." The caregivers had implicit rules which were unyielding.

> The two-year-olds proceeded in a line from their classroom to the gym. Once there, they were directed to line up against the wall, sit on the floor, and wait. They waited, watching another group of children already at play riding bikes, running, and climbing. The caregiver walked over to talk with another adult. Daniel, eager to play, stood up. Before he could move, the caregiver yelled from across the room (about twenty feet), "I didn't tell you you could get up. Sit down!" A few minutes later, still from across the room, she called to them, "OK, you can get up now!" The toddlers jumped up and ran to play.

In this last situation the caregiver's rationale was unclear. While the children waited, she made no preparations for their play; she was not waiting for the first group to leave the area, as they remained. It appears that her control of the children was arbitrary.

Caregivers intervene in and control children's play beyond imposing prohibitions. At times they become overinvolved, in misguided attempts to direct children's actions, as in the following situation.

> The caregiver had set out paper and a box of pastel markers on a table so that the children could draw pictures. Jeff (two years) was at the table drawing with a light blue marker. He put down the marker and walked over to the shelves where there were some more markers. He selected a black marker and returned to the table, where he started drawing in black. The caregiver moved quickly to the table and anxiously said, "Oh, Jeff, where did you get that?" She gestured toward the other markers on the table and said, "These are the markers we are using." She pulled the black marker out of his hand. She then handed him the light blue marker saying, "Use this one." Ignoring this, Jeff instead reached for a purple marker lying on the table. The caregiver grabbed his hand and said, "That's for someone else. The blue one is yours." The other two children at the table each had a marker in hand, and additional markers lay on the table unclaimed.

In this situation Jeff attempted to engage in purposeful, self-directed activity. But his intentionality, even as it did not interfere with or create problems for the other children, created one for the caregiver. Jeff's individuality and unique creativity were secondary to the values of the adult caregiver. By dictating what color markers Jeff could use, the caregiver exerted her power over him, reducing his own power to choose, act, and create. The following field notes also demonstrate the caregivers' power as they impose upon children's play.

> Today the toddlers were sponge painting paper precut into tulip shapes. Zach, surveying his choice of paint colors, decided he wanted to use the brown paint. The caregiver supervising the activity asked her co-worker if she should "let" Zach use the brown paint. They decided to allow Zach to use that color, but the caregiver added to him, "Don't paint the flower too dark, otherwise it will look out of place." On the parents' bulletin board posting "news of the day" was a notice: "We chose our own colors today when we sponge-painted."

> After breakfast, the babies were placed on the rug for "free play." Then, one by one, the caregiver interrupted their play, picking an infant up and taking him or her over to the table to do an "art" project. When it was his or her designated turn, the child had to go with the adult, regardless of whether he or she was already involved in play. As each child sat at the table, the caregiver dipped a brush into paint, placed the brush in each child's hand, and held the child's hand while he or she "painted." When the caregiver felt the picture had been painted enough, the picture was considered finished. In spite of the adult direction, some children showed quite a bit of interest in the painting activity, and were upset when told they had to stop. Each child was allowed to do only one painting.

RESISTANCE

Foucault (1988) posited that power is not completely controlling, that there is always the possibility of resistance in the relations of power (p. 12). Likewise, Goffman also believed that persons simultaneously embrace and resist institutional rules and expectations. But both these writers were referring to adults. What freedom does the young *child* have to project him- or herself into the organization of the day care world? The following field notes describe what may happen when children attempt to resist the caregivers' control and power.

The caregiver had gathered the children (two-year-olds) to-gether on the carpet for a story before lunch. About halfway through the story, she stopped reading and told Caleb to go wash his hands and face. He shook his head and said "No!" The caregiver told Caleb he had to go. He protested again. She put down her book, picked Caleb up, and carried him to the bathroom. Caleb struggled through-out this process, during which I suggested to the caregiver, "Maybe he wants to hear the rest of the story." She responded, "His face is dirty. He has to wash up." The other children waited for the caregiver to return. When they returned to the group, the caregiver resumed reading the story, interrupting herself periodically to call on other chil-dren to wash up.

Corrine's fussiness suggested to the caregiver that she might be hungry for her afternoon bottle. When it was ready, the care-giver held Corrine (three months) in her lap while sitting on the floor. Corrine took the bottle readily, but after she had drunk about three ounces she began to refuse the bottle, turning away her head. The caregiver tried to get Corrine to take more, but Corrine fussed and cried. The caregiver waited a minute or so, removing the bottle, and then tried again. At one point it seemed Corrine had begun to drink again, but I noticed that she was not swallowing, as formula was run-ning down the side of her face toward her ear. I pointed this out to the caregiver. She responded, "Oh well, I'm not stopping now." She con-tinued to hold the bottle in Corrine's mouth. After a few more minutes the caregiver stopped; the bottle was just about empty.

In this last situation, although the caregiver initially took her cues from the infant in responding to indications of hunger, she failed to continue to follow Corrine's cues. She essentially at-tempted to force-feed her and Corrine's only power to resist was to let the formula run out of her mouth. As in the field notes be-low, "the slightest departures from correct behavior are subject to punishment" (Foucault, 1975/1979a, p. 178).

Jonah seems to be a somewhat fidgety baby who, based on previous observations, seems to prefer only certain caregivers to hold him. Today, as it was time for his bottle, the caregiver tried to sit him on her lap. But Jonah arched his back and refused to be still. The caregiver tried putting him in an infant seat, but he arched his back there, too, refusing to sit. So the caregiver laid Jonah on the carpet, but refused to give him his bottle there. She told me the rule was that babies were fed only in laps or in infant seats.

After playing in the large motor room the toddlers were allowed to get drinks of water. When a child asked for a drink but hadn't lined up "right," however, a drink was prohibited. Only the children that lined up were allowed a drink. Henry and Matt were still on bikes when the other children lined up for drinks. When they got to the fountain they were told to go into the classroom, without a drink.

Everyday after lunch the children brush their teeth. Only two children can fit at the sink at a time, so the others that are waiting are expected to sit still and be quiet until it is their turn to brush their teeth. Today (and yesterday) Scott was scolded for not sitting "nicely" until his turn came. He had been kicking the underside of the table as he sat and waited, setting off the other toddlers in imitation. Scott and his followers were called last to the sink and refused help once there.

There are times when a toddler resists sitting in his or her chair during mealtime. Several of them like to get up in the middle of snack and leave the table, so the caregivers decided to strap the toddlers to their chairs during meals and snacks. The caregivers used either a blanket or an elastic cord to wrap around the child and the back of the chair. Or, they took the child's shirt and put it over the back of the chair while still worn by the child; this put the chair between the child's skin and shirt. Within a week after they started strapping the infants in, fifteen-month-old Troy deduced that being belted to the chair didn't mean that he and the chair couldn't move, and he and his chair walked away (or scooted away) from the table. Troy and the other children thought this was really funny, and it got even harder to get the toddlers to stay at the table during snack time.

Today at nap time Emily (nineteen months) was having trouble getting settled. She often has a difficult time falling asleep, tossing and babbling. Once she is sleeping, though, she'll sleep a long time. Today, the caregiver walked over to Emily's cot, grabbed her arm and very roughly turned her on her stomach. She then rubbed Emily's back very hard, while Emily cried. When Emily tried to move, the caregiver pushed down on her back a little harder to stop Emily from moving.

The repression of children's efforts at resistance, critical to the development of their autonomy, leaves them in a kind of "culture of silence" (Freire, 1985, p. 72) where the oppressed are mute, prohibited from "naming" and transforming their world (Freire, 1970, p. 76).[2] This silence is a "failure of understanding" (Silvers, 1983, p. 96); these caregivers stand outside the circle of interpretation and understanding which would allow them to perceive and respond to the children's experiences of the imposed regime. Insofar as children's expressions of their physical and emotional needs and inclinations are subordinate to the adult-imposed schedule, they are silenced. Indeed, the physical management of children is violent when the adults tie them to their chairs and use force to obtain compliance. "In the inner temporality of violence all that is sought is the physical imposing of one's will on the will and body of another" (Denzin, 1984, p. 182). The control of time and children's bodies in time and space amounts to "a systematic negation of self-affirmation and an education toward conformity and docility" (Suransky, 1977, p. 136).

EXTRACTIVE VERSUS
DEVELOPMENTAL POWER

I do not deny that child rearing involves coercion. Child-centered as he was, Rousseau's (1762/1979) benevolent manipulation of Emile was a coercive strategy, as his wants and actions were shaped by his "tutor."[3] As Suransky (1977) noted, "the social reality of child care is such that it is the adults who are imbued with the use and abuse of power in the world of the child" (p. 251). As Guttentag (1987) also pointed out,

> Clearly, parents and other caretakers impose experiences upon children and demand behaviors of children that children find adversive, and equally often experiences that are withheld that children would prefer. . . . However, these actions on the part of caretakers are taken with the reasonable belief that the actions are important for the children's long-term well-being. (p. 21)

It is helpful here to consider Janet Smith's (1983) distinction between "developmental" and "extractive power" (p. 200). Developmental power supports a child's ability to develop his or her own capacities. Likewise, Kuykendall (1983) describes "transformative power" (pp. 264-65) as primarily nurturing, healing, and creative, and I would add, empowering. This includes the possibility of imposing appropriate constraints, which can be empowering. Developmental, transformative power emphasizes interdependence and recognition of individuality, and potential reciprocity, as children are regarded as developing persons. The caregivers' authority does not have to be conceptualized in opposition to the children's developing autonomy.[4] Extractive power, on the other hand, treats children as property or things to be managed, directed, dominated, and controlled. So it is not the exercise of power per se to which I object, but the arbitrary, harsh, and unfeeling exercise of power that I find disturbing.

The management of these child "inmates" (Goffman, 1961, p. 91) might be rationalized in terms of child-rearing aims—that is, helping children learn to live in society—in which case their compliance may be viewed as an indication of developmental progress. In the situations I've described, however, it is extractive, not developmental, power that is exercised, as control appears to have become the operative and primary goal for caregivers, rather than a means to achieving developmental goals, such as health, safety, and competence. Indeed, the field notes illustrate how the exercise of control often operates to the children's detriment, as they are denied drinking water in punishment and repressed in the expression and development of their personal autonomy. The absence of nurturance and compassion characterizes the caregivers' power as destructive.

In the following pages I present a picture for the reader of one child's daily experiences, a succession of epiphanic moments, as she is subjected to the caregivers' power. I go on to discuss the implications of such problematic daily experiences for the children in care.

A DAY IN THE LIFE OF A TODDLER

Arrival

Callie (fifteen months) was new to the center. When her mother brought her into the classroom, Callie, clinging tightly to her mother, had to be pried off of her; her mother left as soon as this was done. Callie was held and comforted for a few minutes and then left alone on the floor where she lay down and cried. When the practicum student attempted to attend to Callie, she was told not to pay "special attention" to her; that would "spoil her and other children will get jealous."

"Free Play"

All the toddlers were directed to the carpet as they finished getting their drinks of water at the fountain. The caregiver reached for two bins of toys that were on some high shelves and emptied them onto the carpet. "Let's play with popbeads," she said, grabbing several pieces and assembling them. "Can you make a chain?" she asked, as she held hers up for the children to see. The ten toddlers were to share the beads; play with the other toys was prohibited. Meanwhile, Callie and another toddler rose from the carpet and moved toward the housekeeping area. The caregiver, seeing this, pulled them by their arms back to the group, "Come on over to the rug, why don't you?" The children complied and did nothing for several seconds. Then they both stood up again and moved towards the housekeeping area. The caregiver again redirected them to the popbeads. She pulled them down as she twice said, "Can you sit down?" At this moment another child, who had not been playing with the popbeads, but watching, got up to play inside the housekeeping area. He was yanked away by the arm, and then all the children were directed to clean up the beads. Brandon, however, continued to play with some beads. The caregiver turned to him and loudly yelled, "Now!" Callie, upon hearing the caregiver, echoed her, "Now!" imitating her tone.

Transition

The transition from play time to snack time was managed by gathering the toddlers together in a group for a story. The children were dismissed one by one, as the story reader called each toddler by name and excused him or her to the snack table. As they waited, the children's faces looked puzzled, perhaps wondering who could go next. Callie, in anticipation, stood up twice to move to the tables, but was directed to sit down until her name was called.

Snack

The toddlers sat at the tables. The caregiver stood over them with a basket of graham crackers. She handed each child one cracker; children were not allowed to help themselves. Callie started to eat hers. The caregiver told her, "wait until everyone has one before you eat yours." The children waited, watching the caregiver. Once the children were served she said, "OK, you can eat now." As they nibbled their crackers she poured them each some milk into paper cups. Callie lifted her cup for a drink, but her grasp crushed the paper and the milk spilled over. The caregiver said, "No more milk for *those who spill it." Callie looked at her with an unhappy expression, but said nothing.*

Transition

The children were just getting up from ten minutes of "quiet time." The caregiver instructed the children to put their pillows away. She told them that they were going for a walk. Callie asked the caregiver "why?" the class was going for a walk. The caregiver responded, "Because we want to."

Teacher-Directed Activity

The children were making squirrels to decorate the room. The caregiver had cut out the shapes two days earlier. Yesterday each child had painted one squirrel brown. Today they were to glue cotton balls to their tails. It was now Callie's turn. She stood next to the caregiver as the caregiver applied some glue to the paper tail. The caregiver then reached into the bag of cotton balls and took out five, which she handed to Callie, who had been standing by. Callie took one ball and tried several times to stick it to the unglued part of the squirrel. "Here, Callie," the caregiver directed as she placed one of the cotton balls on the tail. She took Callie's hand in hers to pat the cotton down. She then placed another cotton ball into Callie's hand, who repeated her earlier "mistake." The caregiver repeated her direction, again, physically manipulating Callie's hand, until all five cotton balls were on the tail. "You're finished!" the caregiver exclaimed, "Go and play." She then called for Loren, who came eagerly over. By the time she arrived, the caregiver was busily gluing her squirrel's tail. Loren reached for the glue stick. The caregiver pulled it away from her and said, "It's not your turn." Loren waited. When it was time for her to stick on the cotton, she followed the same pattern as Callie. After a few minutes she asked, "Why are we making this?" The caregiver responded, "It's fun because you get to glue cotton balls on."

Lunchtime

Callie was sitting at the table between the student and the caregiver. She kept closing her eyes and her head was nodding back and forth; she was obviously very tired. The student asked her, "Callie, do you want to go to sleep?" She opened her eyes, looked at the student, and said, "yeah." The caregiver intervened, saying, "No, not until after fruit." Then she tried to put a spoonful of tuna casserole in Callie's mouth while saying, "Eat some more tuna, Callie." Callie turned her head away. Then the caregiver said, "Callie, if you don't eat any tuna, you won't get any fruit." Callie did not respond, she looked straight ahead with a blank expression. The caregiver rose from the table to serve fruit to the other children, except Callie, saying to her, "no fruit for you, Callie." Again, Callie did not respond, as she was falling asleep again. After the caregiver finished eating her own fruit, she cleaned up Callie and told her "Go lay down, now."

Nap

Callie woke up from her nap after about one hour; the other children were still sleeping. She sat up, rubbed her eyes, and looked about her. From across the room, the caregiver called, "Lie down! Nap is not over yet!" Callie complied, occassionally sitting up and looking about her.

Snack

Children were called to the snack tables one by one. They waited, as the caregiver stood over them, dropping in front of each child a handful of Cheerios cereal. The adults did not sit down and join the children at the table, but hovered over the children while they ate. Children were not allowed their glasses of milk until they were done with the dry cereal.

Toileting

The children were finishing their snack. The caregiver announced it was "potty time." Four potty-chairs were placed in the classroom, outside the bathroom where there is only one toilet. Children were called over to sit on the chairs. "Callie, I need you to go potty." Callie, still sitting at the table, ignored the caregiver's command. "Callie, NOW!" said the caregiver as she approached Callie and led her to the toilet.

Afternoon Teacher-Directed Activity

It was time to implement a planned activity—messing about with shaving cream. The caregiver called three toddlers at a time over to the table. She observed aloud that there was one child in the

*class who did not like to get her hands dirty, but she could not re-
member exactly who it was. After a while it was Callie's turn to come
up to the table. The caregiver looked at me and said she thought it
was Callie. She proceeded to put a smock on Callie and spray some
shaving cream down in front of her on the table. For a minute or so
Callie just looked at it and did not touch it. No one said anything to
her. After a minute, the caregiver, without asking, took Callie's hands
and put them into the shaving cream, saying, "Go like this, Callie."
She then walked away. Callie turned to the practicum student and
said that she was "done." The student said, "okay," and suggested
she go ahead and get cleaned up. The caregiver, returning to the
scene, intercepted Callie and said, "Well, Callie isn't finished. Come
on, Callie, make a picture." The student told her that she had said it
was okay for Callie to go and wash up. The caregiver looked at her
for a minute, without replying, and then told Callie to come with her
back to the table. Callie complied, with a confused and distressed
expression on her face as she looked back at the student.*

Departure

*It was about 5:15 P.M. The room was cleaned up and the toys
put away. The few toddlers still here stood at the windows and doors
and gazed out. The caregiver watched them silently. Both the caregiver and the children appeared tired and eager to go home. They
awaited the arrival of the parents. The caregiver saw through the
window Callie's mom pulling into the parking lot. She quickly dressed
Callie in her coat and got her ready to go.*

CHILDREN'S PLACE IN THE
SOCIAL WORLD OF DAY CARE

The parameters allowing children their own activity and
intentionality are severely constrained in these child care centers.
The infants and toddlers described here are individual in their
development and personality, yet their individual differences and
preferences often have no influence in the caregivers' management of routines and the exercise of power. Each child, in his
or her management, seems interchangable with any other. As
Foucault (1975/1979a) wrote, "in discipline, the elements are
interchangeable, since each is defined by the place it occupies in

a series . . ." (p. 145). Indeed, changes in classroom grouping are typically made according to quantitative (not individual, or even developmental) criteria such as maximum group size and children's chronological ages. Every six or twelve months children move on to the next (older) age group and assume the routines of those children previously there. "It is a perpetual movement in which individuals replace one another in a space marked off by aligned invervals" (Foucault, 1975/ 1979a, p. 147). The structure remains unchanged by the particular children present.

Over time it seemed that problems with control and disciplinary power emerged more frequently and more intensely as infants grew into toddlerhood and beyond. It is as if the *fact* of the toddlers' emerging and increasing mobility, as well as their initiative, intentionality, and autonomy, *necessitated* the caregivers' control. As Polakow (1992) observed, "the spontaneous, moving, energetic playing being of the child presents a threat" (p. 176) to the disciplinary structure of the program and hence needs to be contained. Spontaneity, emotionality, and playfulness are "antinorms detrimental to the imposed spatial and temporal structure" (Polakow, 1992, p. 176).

As caregivers face the constant, unpredictable, and demanding needs of the children, they may feel a sense of diminishing control and the loss of their own individual autonomy. They may be driven to exert control where they can—on powerless children. The caregivers' inflexibility, then, may stem partly from their own needs for control and predictability. Recall how, in the field notes on page 29, the caregiver didn't want "too many" toys out, as if that would contribute to a more chaotic situation. The field notes below suggest that caregivers may feel that to give up control is to be out of control, so they relentlessly pursue it to control their own anxiety.

Before the children arrived the caregivers had filled a shallow tray with cornmeal and placed scoops in it. They covered the tray with a small blanket and placed it on the floor underneath the storage shelves. They planned to introduce this activity after snack time. Later, during the morning play time, Sandy and several other children discovered the tray, unnoticed by the caregivers, and began scooping cornmeal out of it into other containers on the floor. After some time, the caregiver became aware of this activity and exclaimed, "Look what you've done! You're making a mess!" The second caregiver then added, "Jackie had that all set up for after snack and now

*you've gone and ruined it! Sandy, do you have to ruin everything?"
The first caregiver picked Sandy up off the floor and started brushing
the cornmeal off of him, all the while telling him that he had ruined the
activity planned for later.*

Caregivers' implementation of the daily schedule is intended to make the day easier, more managable, and efficient for *them*, as well as the children. They may be doing the best they can, given the situations within which they find themselves, unprepared, and from which they can find no way out (Mills, 1959). They fail to see how their strictly enforced routinization works against them, pitting them in struggles with the children, which they respond to, in turn, with more rules and disciplinary punishment. The caregivers themselves undoubtedly experienced the same "discipline" as grade school children (the only model for group care they may have to draw upon).[5] It is "a machine in which everyone is caught, those who exercise power just as much as those over whom it is exercised" (Foucault, 1980, p. 156). In Mills' (1959) words, caregivers are "caught in the limited milieux of their everyday lives . . . without any ideas of the ends they serve" (p. 168).

In the situations described throughout this chapter, the experience of childhood is not, as conventionally perceived, "a time of carefree disorganized bliss" (Denzin, 1977, p. 182). As these infants and toddlers were expected to master physiological, behavioral, and emotional control, "time is not experienced as a spontaneous part of the lived-world but rather as an external force" (Polakow, 1992, p. 65). The field notes show how caregivers and children are not in "concert time" or "temporal togetherness" (Sharron, 1982, pp. 69, 72) despite the amount of time and space they share. Very early, then, children experience power as "an inherent feature of social relations" as power operates to constrain or otherwise direct their actions (Philp, 1985, pp. 74–75). The children's jobs, as they learn to comply to caregiver directives, are

> to be docile and accepting of the teachers' position, playful when play is demanded, sleepy when it is time to go to bed, hungry when meals are served. . . . *Not to get it right* at an early age is to place oneself in an untenable position—in a position where whether you want to or not, you must get it right. (Denzin, 1973a, p. 17)

This is how these day care centers teach children how to be children as well as their place in the social world.

SUMMARY

In this chapter I have presented field notes that describe the caregivers' exercise of power over the children in space and time, particularly in the management of daily routines and control of their play. I conclude that caregivers' need for control and their incessant, intrusive, and extractive practice of discipline suppresses the children's emerging autonomy and empowerment. In the following chapter I go on to suggest that these children's emotional understandings are also severely affected by the relations of power.

4
Emotion

We are dedicated to creating and maintaining a warm, nurturing atmosphere that provides for unpressured learning
through play. . . .

—*Day care program brochure*

The experience of lived space and time is relational. The
day-care space is an interpersonal context in which children feel
and express their emotions, and interpret their emotional experiences.[1] The emotional culture of these day-care settings is a central feature of the problematic relations of power thus far
described. Emotional culture is "a group's set of daily beliefs, vocabulary, regulative norms, and other ideational resources per-
taining to emotion" (Gordon, 1989a, p. 322). I would add "daily
practices" to this definition, as they are indicative of these beliefs
and norms.

In this chapter, I extend the interpretation of field notes as
situated emotional interactions. Drawing primarily from Sartre
and Hochschild, I show how the the exercise of power creates emotional epiphanies for the children, and how caregivers objectify
and alienate children and "strip" them of their "child selves"
(Suransky, 1983, p. 154). I discuss how these problematics emerge
as child care, for the caregivers, involves alienated emotional labor. I conclude by expressing the concern that the problematics observed may amount to unsurpassable childhoods for these very
young children, as they construct understandings of themselves,
others, and their worlds in these emotional situations.

OBJECTIFICATION AND SERIALITY

Discipline "makes" individuals; it is the specific technique of a
power that regards individuals both as objects and as instru-
ments of its exercise.

—Foucault, *Discipline and Punish*

The exercise of power, in the situations described thus far,
reveal how (or require that) children are managed as objects. As

51

"not yet persons," children are only "material upon which to work" (Goffman, 1961, pp. 115, 74). As caregivers' *work*, infants in day care become the objects of the caregivers' labor. Children become objectified as their management takes precedence over their existential *being* (Polakow, 1992).

The toddlers were required to be quiet, and sit with their hands in their laps before they were served lunch. They were not allowed or encouraged to serve themselves. Some children were refused food until they stopped making "noise." Some had been crying, others were talking. The adults talked to each other while they served the food and during lunchtime. No reason was given to the children about why they shouldn't talk. When the children's plates were empty, they were given more food, without being asked first. Afterwards, their plates were taken away, also without being consulted.

In these situations, the child's position in the world of day care constitutes his or her immersion in what Sartre called the field of the *practico-inert*:

> In this field, social relations are atomized and fragmented. Individuals are isolated and separated. Their reciprocity is negative and external . . . [they] share a common field of activity but no awareness of each other. (Hirsch, 1982, pp. 75–76)

Caregivers' lack of awareness is indicated by the way they seem to go through the motions of managing children's routines, as if only their bodies and physical needs required attention. Consider the field notes below.

Lena (five months) was sitting on the floor playing with some toys. The caregiver, deciding to change her diaper, approached Lena from behind, abruptly and wordlessly picked her up, and laid her on the changing table. Lena squirmed while being changed. The caregiver did not talk to Lena or give her a toy to hold onto and distract her. A few times Lena gurgled and cooed. The caregiver did not respond. She changed Lena's diaper without looking at her face; the caregiver's movements seemed almost robotic, without expression. When finished with the task, she put Lena back down on the floor, also without a word.

It was late afternoon. I was in a rocker feeding one infant, and another caregiver, Liza, was rocking another baby to sleep. A second caregiver, Dolly, was looking over the daily charts posted on the wall to make sure no one forgot to write anything down. She called out, "Is little Joey asleep?" I looked over at him and told her he was, and had been since 3:00. Dolly said that Joey was supposed to have his bottle by 4:00, so we had better wake him up. Liza suggested, "why not let him sleep? I'll feed him when he wakes up." Dolly replied, "No, he'll wake up crying and then we won't be able to feed him." She went ahead and woke up Joey, who did take his bottle willingly, if sleepily.

In these situations the children's presence had no existential significance for the caregivers. Caregivers interacted *at* rather than *with* children, although they interacted with each other. The field notes below show how caregivers are *externally preoccupied* (Goffman, 1967).

An adult from another classroom walked in and began a conversation with the caregivers, in the presence of the children. When this happened, every child stopped what he or she was doing and turned around to watch the adults. The visit was extended; conversation personal. The adults talked about a wedding shower they had attended, and another caregiver who had gotten drunk. When the children sought attention from the adults, calling to them and tugging on their clothes, attempting to distract them from their conversations, they were ignored or dismissed.

It was nap time. The adults sat in the room and talked with each other. They did not lower their voices. Toddlers who were unable to sleep lay on their cots unattended by the caregivers. As more children started to wake up, the adults continued to sit and talk with each other. The children were required to stay on their cots, silent and waiting.

The children's attempts to communicate with caregivers in these situations were ignored, discounted, or denied. To the extent caregivers are *unconnected with* the children present (Goffman, 1967) and regard them as "nonpersons" (Goffman, 1959), children are objectified.[2] "To be *objectified* by the Other is to be totalized, defined, judged, limited—incorporated into a system of ends that one has not chosen—and at the mercy of an alien consciousness" (Schroeder, 1984, p. 176). The following field notes provide another illustration.

The toddlers were playing in the large motor area. Three caregivers sat on the floor watching the children play. Two-year-old Vicki arrived with her mother, who told the caregivers Vicki had been awake since 3:30 that morning. Vicki sat and absently watched the others; she did not respond to the adults' initiations. Her eyes started to close. One caregiver said to another that if Vicki fell asleep before lunch, she wouldn't sleep during nap time. Suddenly, this caregiver grabbed Vicki from behind and shook her, saying, "Wake up, Vicki, wake up!" Vicki began to cry. The caregiver told her, "but Vicki, if you sleep now, you won't take your nap." Vicki continued to scream and cry. The caregiver said, "Vicki, stop it now, no reason to cry."

In the above situation, Vicki was at the "mercy" of her caregiver who failed to recognize and respond to Vicki's physical and emotional state. Vicki was to be managed according to the "system of ends"—the daily schedule—which had little relation to her own individual needs and choices. In this way, she was objectified, left in "a field of powerlessness and impotence . . . a field of alienation" (Hirsch, 1982, p. 76).

I was sitting on the floor reading books to some of the children when Marissa (twenty-two months) arrived this morning. Apparently her mother left her in the hallway outside the room door and Marissa started screaming. The caregiver brought Marissa into the room and shut the door. Marissa screamed and threw herself on the floor, screaming and kicking. The caregiver matter-of-factly told her to stop crying, but Marissa continued. The caregiver tried to get Marissa's snowsuit off but had a difficult time as Marissa continued to cry and did not cooperate. As the caregiver pulled the last leg off, Marissa arched her back so that she fell backwards onto the floor and hit her head. She screamed even louder then. The caregiver, who had been wordless throughout the undressing, put Marissa's suit away and said, "Stop it already, Marissa." Marissa continued to cry. The second caregiver, who had been sitting nearby at a table cutting paper, rose from her chair and wordlessly grabbed Marissa by her forearm, lifted her off the floor, put her in the hallway, returned to the room without Marissa, slammed the door, and said, "That is so we don't kill her." We could hear Marissa continue to scream through the door. A few minutes later the first caregiver went out to pick up and bring Marissa back into the room. Marissa was left by the door, inside now, screaming. The adults ignored her. I got up and went over to Marissa and asked her, "Would you like me to hold you?" She nodded her head "yes" in response. I picked her up and she immediately

*stopped crying. I continued to comfort her, and eventually engaged
her in some play.*

Undoubtedly this child's separation from her parent was
a stressful one this day, as it often is for toddlers. The mother
might have come into the room with her child, but since she did
not a challenge was presented for the caregivers. While children
experiencing tantrums are often best left alone temporarily, these
caregivers failed to let Marissa know that they were there, emotionally and physically, for her. They could have acknowledged
Marissa's feelings with a simple statement such as, "you're upset
your mom left you in the hall. Come on in and let's see what I can
do to help you to feel better." Instead, the caregivers continued to
manipulate Marissa bodily and reject her emotionally, and then
failed to explain their actions. *The caregivers have the power to
comfort or not.* In *not* comforting, they exert *negative* power, as op-
posed to the healing, nurturing, transformative power described
in the previous chapter.

These situations indicate the primary structure of the
practico-inert: *seriality*. Seriality excludes the relation of reciprocity (Sartre, 1960/1976); there is nothing personal about serial
relations—the "real being" of the individual is disregarded (Hirsh,
1982, p. 76). The series is a field which reduces the individual to
an object. The lack of recognition and reciprocity is suggested
again in the following field notes.

*The caregiver lifted two infants out of their cribs and placed
them on the floor. She put a few toys on the floor in front of them. She
then sat in her chair and proceeded to do some paperwork. The babies played contentedly. The program director walked in and the two
adults began to talk with each other. After a few minutes, Kaitlin
(seven months) crawled over to the caregiver and attempted to explore her papers. The caregiver and director ignored her. Kaitlin tried
to pull herself up the leg of the caregiver. She began to cry. Another
child, just waking up, also began to cry in his crib. The two adults continued to focus on their conversation.*

If either adult in the above situation had recognized and acknowledged Kaitlin, and her overtures for attention, they might
have simply lifted her onto a lap, while they continued their
adult business. Likewise, the infant who had awakened in his
crib might have been picked up and held by one of the adults as
she talked.

Kristen (nine months) fell down and began to cry. She lifted her arms to be held, her eyes brimming with tears. As I reached to pick her up, the caregiver said, "Don't pick her up. We don't need to spoil her." Kristen continued to cry, but the caregivers ignored her.

As I entered the room, Clarke (twelve months) toddled over to me crying, tears streaming down his face. The caregiver was a few feet away, standing over the other five children playing on the carpet. I knelt to talk to Clarke. He reached out his arms to me, still crying. I said, "I think you need a hug," and held him. He quieted and clung to me. This was our first meeting—we were strangers. As I held Clarke, the caregiver matter-of-factly told me he had been crying all morning. She explained that he recently had been at his grandmother's, who, she believed, "held him all the time." She suggested this was why he wanted to be held. But, she told me, she was not going to hold Clarke. When I left for the day I put Clarke down, and he began to cry vehemently again, despite my efforts to comfort him.

In these last two situations the caregivers were aware of the infants' emotional states and needs. They did not seem too busy with other children or tasks, but, as a matter of principle, they refused to respond. An infant's desire to be held was not a reason for caregiver compliance. People respond toward emotions according to the meanings they assign to them (Gordon, 1985; see also Blumer, 1969; Denzin, 1984). The problem here is that, for the caregivers, the children's emotions had no meaning, or certainly little significance, as children were rejected, abandoned, and emotionally isolated.

Jolie (twenty months) asked the practicum student to take her to the bathroom. Once there, the student discovered Jolie's pants were soaking wet. The student removed the toddler's clothes and helped her onto the toilet. While Jolie sat, the student related what happened to the caregiver, asking her to bring over some clean, dry clothing. The caregiver brought the clothes and tossed them on the floor by the child. Jolie looked up at the caregiver, who looked at her with disapproval and anger, saying, "Yuk, Jolie! I don't like what you are doing! Don't go the bathroom in your pants. That is yukky!" She left without waiting for a response. The student finished dressing Jolie, who looked upset and bewildered.

Alex (eighteen months) responded to a conflict by biting another toddler, who promptly returned the bite. The caregiver told Alex that he "deserved" to be bitten. Alex was then punished by being placed in "time out." Afterwards, Alex approached the caregiver, indicating he wanted to be held. The caregiver refused, saying she "didn't want to" hold him.

These last two caregivers did not seem to consider developmental explanations for the children's behavior, nor the consequences of their own responses. For example, biting is, although inappropriate, an age-typical behavior in toddlers with limited verbal ability to express their feelings of anger and frustration. Toileting is a skill that emerges over time and has as much to do with a child's physical development and ability as it does with her willingness to comply. The adults' responses did not help the children to understand or change their behavior. Moreover, they refused to acknowledge and respond to these children's feelings or to explain their actions. When caregivers are not responsive, children's self-feelings, and thus their *selves*, are denied legitimation.

Punishment, by way of rejection, withholding of affection, refusal to forgive and comfort, isolation, and "time out," was a common response of caregivers to children's emotional expressions, as in this episode:

Paul (two years) was brought crying and screaming to the infant room. Apparently he had been spitting. The caregiver told him that if he was going to "act like a baby then you will be with the babies." She left him in a corner of the room by the changing table, where he continued to cry and shake. Another caregiver continued to call him a baby.

In this situation the caregivers failed not only to offer support and understanding, but shamed and punished this child for expressing his emotions.[3] Like Alex, who sought understanding, forgiveness, and comfort, the children in these situations have, in essence, been emotionally abandoned.

The toddlers were playing, except for Kyle (fifteen months) who was crying. As the toddler approached her, the caregiver knelt down, put her hands on Kyle's shoulders, and said, "You must learn to smile. You're always crying. I'm not picking you up." She walked away from Kyle. He followed her and reached out to hold onto her leg. The caregiver, exasperated, said, "Will you just go away? Turn it off. I don't want to hear it." The child continued to stand there and cry.

The "emotion work" (Hochschild, 1983, p. 7) this caregiver expected from Kyle—learn to smile on demand; suppress your negative emotions—is developmentally inappropriate and emotionally insensitive, and fails to help him understand his emotions as he learns to manage them. That toddlers *can* learn to control their emotions, or emotional expressions, to some extent is not disputed. The issue is whether adults *ought* to expect toddlers to control their emotions, in what ways, under what circumstances, and with what understandings and consequences. Also, in these field notes, the fact that this toddler is a *boy* may be influencing the caregivers' expectations that it is inappropriate for him to cry.

The situations with Paul and Kyle suggest that caregivers are primarily interested in children's surface behaviors, not their feelings, as they manage them (Power, 1985b). Children's emotional beings, their emotional expressions, and their responses appear irrelevant. As a result, children's emotions were ignored, suppressed, denied, and left unclarified—but they may have learned to "get it right" all the same; that is, they eventually learn to reconstruct their behavior and emotional expressions in accord with the caregivers' demands.

Crying is a major way nonverbal infants and toddlers express their feelings. They need to know they are accepted by adults even when they cry. But these caregivers often seemed to have little tolerance for children's crying, as the field notes below also illustrate.

Two infants began to cry in their cribs, where they had been put because they were "fussing." One caregiver said to another, "I wish we could lose them."

Letitia (eight months) had been laying on the carpet playing. After a while she started to cry. The caregiver, who was not involved with other infants, yelled from her chair, "Letitia! Be quiet!" Startled, she stopped crying momentarily, but began again. No one made another effort to calm her. I finally decided to pick her up myself, which quieted her.

Kara (four months) was crying. She lifted her arms up to me, her eyes brimming with tears. As I reached down to her, the caregiver said to me, "Don't pick her up. She does that to everyone at first. We don't need to spoil her." Kara continued to cry. I hugged her briefly and then tried to interest her in a toy. She continued to cry. The caregivers ignored her.

Kara may "do that to everyone at first," that is, reach out to every adult newcomer in the classroom, because she may have learned her primary caregivers are emotionally unavailable to her. She continues to reach out to other adults in the search for one to whom she can turn to for emotional sustenance and comfort. As Reynolds (1990) wrote,

> Holding, patting, stroking, and hugging are very real physical [and emotional] needs of the young child. Adults sometimes discount this need by labeling behavior as "looking for attention." The term "discounting," when referring to feelings, means to diminish and disregard the amount and intensity of feelings, making them seem less important than they are. (p. 79)

Rory (seventeen months) cried as his mother left the room. His crying escalated as he pressed his face to the window in the door. Occassionally he turned around to look at the two caregivers, who ignored him. Rory's face and eyes were red. After ten minutes a caregiver went and stood over him, commanding, "Calm down!" Rory stopped crying, looked at her, she looked at him, and he resumed his crying. She told him again to calm down. He continued to cry. She walked away, saying "someone take me out of here!" After another fifteen minutes the center director, having noticed the scene through the windows, entered the room and picked up and held Rory. He quieted immediately. She stayed with him, and after a few minutes was able to interest him in some toys. Still teary-eyed and whimpering, he gradually responded.

In this instance, one caregiver (the director) was willing to attend to and comfort Rory, illustrating the power of a responsive caregiver to calm, soothe, and redirect an unhappy toddler. This only occurred however, after an extended period of inattention and rejection, and expressions of impatience by his primary caregiver.

Janine (eleven months) was standing at her crib reaching into it through the bars. She was whimpering quietly. The longer she stood there the more frustrated she became. I walked over and saw that she was reaching for her pacifier. When I gave it to her, the caregiver took it away, saying she couldn't have it. Janine began to cry. When I asked the caregiver why Janine wasn't allowed to have her pacifier, she explained it was because Janine would share it with the other babies. To prevent this she was only allowed to have her pacifier in her crib. Although Janine continued to cry, she was not placed in her crib with the pacifier, or given a substitute object. Neither did the caregiver attempt to distract her by inviting her to play.

The situations throughout this text describe human beings not essentially oriented toward others, rather, caregivers, as managers, are, for the most part, emotionally disengaged. Their emotional disengagement inhibits their abilities to comprehend and respond to the perspectives of the children. This inability, in turn, further disengages them from the children. As Hochschild (1983) wrote, "it is from feeling that we learn the self-relevance of what we see, remember, or imagine" (p. 196). "When we lose access to feeling, we lose a central means of interpreting the world around us" (p. 188). The field notes below illustrate how caregivers' emotional disengagement can result in discrepant interpretations or spurious emotional understandings (Denzin, 1984) of the children's emotional expressions.

Selena (eight months) had been up for about an hour now, after a three hour nap. She started to "get cranky," fussing and whimpering. The caregiver checked her diaper, which was dry. Selena had had a bottle thirty minutes before, so hunger was dismissed. The caregivers decided that Selena was tired and put her back to bed. It did not seem to occur to them to play with Selena.

The children were getting up from their naps. While the caregiver was putting on Jamie's socks, Patsy (twenty-three months) approached her, her face red from crying. The caregiver noted her crying, but said she could not figure out what Patsy wanted. She did not pick up and hold Patsy or try to distract her with a toy or a snack. After a long period of continued crying and screaming, the caregiver decided to check Patsy's temperature to see if that had anything to do with her behavior. Patsy did not have a temperature, but the caregiver decided to call Patsy's mother to have her take Patsy to the doctor.

CHILD CARE AS
EMOTIONAL LABOR

Noddings (1984) observed that "when we move beyond the natural circles of caring, we may begin to feel burdened" (p. 52); "natural affection and receptivity break down" (pp. 74–75).[4] To whatever extent the caring capacity may be "natural" and desired among caregivers, it is often thwarted in the day-care setting. For those for whom it is a job, child *care* is transformed into child management. As the caregivers' job, any emotional responsiveness becomes emotional labor—the publicly observable management of feelings sold for a wage (Hochschild, 1983).[5]

> This labor requires one to induce or suppress feeling in order to sustain the outward countenance that produces the proper state of mind in others—in this case, the sense of being cared for in a convivial and safe place. (p. 7)

And it is this *labor* wherein lies the potential for estrangement and alienation from self and others. Consider the field notes below.

Today's snack was chunks of fresh fruit. The caregiver tossed the food across the table to the children she couldn't reach from her seat. Her only words to them were directions to sit still and finish eating. Jake had just awoken from his nap and was hungry for his bottle. The caregiver left him in his crib while she prepared the formula. She then propped the bottle on the blanket so it would stay in Jake's mouth without her holding onto it. She returned to her rocker and read her novel.

The emotional labor of the caregivers is complex, as they are expected to develop a sense of investment in each child that enables them to sustain caring throughout each day and over time, but also each day release children to their parents. In short, caregivers are expected to emotionally engage intensely, and disengage gracefully, and do both upon demand (Zigler & Lang, 1991).

The child's contribution to the caring relationship may not be enough to sustain the most well-intentioned caregiver's capacities for caregiving. "Children cannot reciprocate care equally, they require a degree of selflessness and attention that is specific to them" (Grimshaw, 1986, p. 253). To be other-directed for such long hours can create considerable emotional strain on caregivers' capacities to care for the children. Moreover, in contrast to family-based child rearing, the infants in child care never appear to grow up, or out of their physical and emotional dependency upon their adult caregivers. This is because as infants in day care get older, they (typically) are moved into new classrooms and replaced by younger infants. As children move on, caregivers' opportunities to take pleasure in what has been described as the child's "revealing of self" (Noddings, 1984, p. 73) as they grow are limited.

In contrast to the mutual caring possible in adult relationships, child care by necessity involves predominantly one-way nurturing relationships in which the adult is the nurturing caregiver and the child is the one who is cared for and nurtured (Klein, 1989). The pleasure may seem to belong all to the cared for with little left for the caregiver—who may feel "conned" by the mythical lure of emotionally satisfying child caregiving (Rose, 1986). Given these observations, and those described in the field notes, it is not surprising (but sadly ironic) that in one of the few studies examining working conditions in day care centers that one-fourth of the caregivers mentioned dealing with children as something they liked least about their job (Kontos & Stremmel, 1988, p. 88)!

The caregiver sat Linnie (five months) in the high chair. She sat there contentedly as the caregiver silently fed her cereal and fruit, and then complacently took her bottle. After Linnie finished eating, the caregiver put some toys on the tray and left Linnie in the high chair. The caregiver sat by herself in the rocker. (Two other babies were sleeping, and I was playing the others.) Linnie played with the toys for a little while, but then indicated she wanted to get down. When the caregiver did not respond, Linnie dropped the toys one by one off the tray, watching them fall to the ground. Then she started to cry. The caregiver wordlessly picked the toys up and put them back on the tray. Linnie knocked them off again and cried. The caregiver again put the toys back on the tray. This repeated one more time, at which point I said to the caregiver, "It looks like Linnie wants to get down and play." The caregiver replied that "Linnie is just so spoiled that she needs constant attention." But she took Linnie out of her high chair and sat her on the carpet. She refused, however, to interact with her.

The caregiver was hovering over Andrea's crib, vigorously shaking it. (The crib was not built for rocking.) Andrea (seven months) was curled up into a ball in the corner of her crib, crying. The caregiver continued to shake her crib for about ten minutes. She then picked up Andrea and put her on the tile floor in front of the crib. She said, "If you won't go to sleep, then you can just sit there," and then walked away. (Another child's parents were in the room observing this.) A while later, Andrea was rubbing her eyes as she lay on the floor. The caregiver picked her up and changed her diaper. She took Andrea and laid her in her crib. Andrea instantly began to cry. The caregiver began to shake the crib. This continued for a while. The caregiver did not talk soothingly to Andrea or pat her back. Another caregiver came over and observed the situation. She picked Andrea up and sat with her in the rocking chair. In about ten minutes Andrea fell asleep. This caregiver then placed her gently in her crib where she continued to sleep.

Caregiver "burnout" and its effects on the quality of care has been noted before (Maslach & Pines, 1977; Whitebook, Howes, Darrah, & Friedman, 1982). Maslach and Pines (1977) described the dehumanization process in which caregivers' awareness of others and their feelings decreases as they attempt to cope with the emotional stresses of their work. Caregivers react passively, stop caring, and become remote and detached (Hochschild, 1983). They may withhold themselves and their own emotionality as an act of self-protection.

CHILD CARE AS
ALIENATED LABOR

For the child care workers described here, then, caregiving may be alienated labor (Marx, 1844/1983).[6] Alienated labor is a set of responses resulting from specific kinds of social arrangements (which include day care centers). It is one outcome of workers' lack of control over their labor, absence of pleasure and well-being in their labor, and, in this case, perhaps lack of respect from society for the work that they do. Caregivers are often excluded from the decision-making processes of the program administration (Benson, n.d.), such as when infants are to be moved on into new rooms, or the number of infants for whom the caregivers will be responsible. Caregiver practices may evolve partly in attempts to resist the practical constraints imposed on them. As caregivers face the constant, unpredictable, and demanding needs of the children, in working for others, they may feel a sense of diminishing control and the loss of their own individual autonomy.

Child care workers experience their "alienation in the form of powerlessness, meaninglessness, isolation and self-estrangement" (Gintis, 1972, p. 3). Child care is one of the lowest paid occupations in the United States (Modigliani, 1986). Caregivers' days are filled with the drudgery of routine tasks such as diaper changing and feeding which are repeated endlessly. Seldom noted are the occupational hazards that affect caregivers' physical well-being, for example, strain from frequent lifting of children and exposure to infectious diseases. The constant crying of several infants does create stress, which may manifest itself in headaches and upset stomachs (Reynolds, 1990), in addition to the emotional withdrawal noted here. Caregivers may work with one or two other adults but are generally isolated from adult society, as the children demand their attention.[7] The competing and simultaneous demands placed on caregivers, as well as the lack of personal and institutional resources to meet them, compounds the problematics of negotiating care.

Alienation is both failure and estrangement (Schwalbe, 1986). It is a mode of disengagement (Goffman, 1967). As alienated emotional labor, child caregiving precludes recognition of both the caregivers' and the children's emotional selves.[8] Insofar as caregivers fail to perceive, comprehend, and respond to the children's behaviors and emotional expressions, and are unable to enter into reciprocal relations with the children for whom they care, not recognizing themselves or their own childhoods in the children, caregivers' "exhausting labor" (Sartre, 1960/1963, p. 13) is alienated and alienating. The caregivers' alienation is transferred to the children, as they experience their alienation in the work of the alienated caregiver.[9]

Two caregivers sat on the floor with four infants. Another child, Alan (seven months), crawled over to them, excited. One caregiver said to him, "no, I don't want you—you weigh a ton. No, Alan, you tub, get out of the way!" Then she said, "Go to Martha" [the other caregiver]. When Alan looked toward Martha, she said to him, "No-o-o, not me Alan, just stay there." Alan looked confused. Then the first caregiver lifted him into the playpen and said, "You play in here, Alan," and turned away. Alan tried to climb out of the playpen, but retreated when he was yelled at.

The caregiver was giving Brad (six months) his afternoon bottle. Brad was in an infant seat on a small table and the caregiver was seated in a chair beside it holding onto the bottle. Brad was drinking his milk slowly, gazing at the ceiling where mobiles hung. The caregiver repeatedly jabbed the bottle in and out of Brad's mouth and moved it back and forth, saying, "Come on, Brad, you're not the only baby in the world or in this room. Stop messing around and get to drinking."

As the field notes above illustrate, child care work, as alienated emotional labor, becomes a site of hostile and painful feelings in which the caregiver confronts the child as a hostile object (Rose, 1986). The estrangement, alienation, and hostility felt by caregivers is indicated not only in their exercise of negative power—the ways they control, punish, and ignore children—but also by the statements they have made, excerpted from field notes included throughout this chapter, and presented below:

> *That is so we don't kill her.*
> *Will you just go away? Turn it off. I don't want to hear it.*
> *I wish we could lose them.*
> *Be quiet!*
> *Someone take me out of here!*
> *I don't want you . . . get out of the way!*

The phenomenon of emotionally alienated caregivers is an ironic and stark contrast to the picture of day care offered to parents in program brochures. Consider the following phrases which appear repeatedly in these brochures, promoting a mythology of loving care:

> Caring adults. . . .
> An atmosphere of warmth and trust. . . .
> Daily routines are carried out with the focus on nurturing. . . .
> Children are safe, loved. . . .
> A warm, nurturing atmosphere. . . .
> Caregivers show genuine concern for each and every child. . . .
> We make sure that learning is an absolute joy. . . .
> A warm, loving and secure environment. . . .

To the extent mother love is a commodity to be sold, day care is, in some sense, one more example of the commercialization of human feeling firmly entrenched in our culture (Hochschild, 1983). The work of child care may be seen as one more example of the alienating and self-destructive emotional fields of experience confronting persons in our society (Denzin, 1984). The myth of freely given, abundant love breaks down, as infant day care involves a move "from the known world of intimates to the unknown world of biographical strangers" (Loseke & Cahill, n.d., p. 3).

> Regardless of the ideal that [caregivers] should be mothers who love the children they care for, economic transactions transform [them] into employees and necessarily distinguish them from mothers. (Loseke, 1989, p. 323)[10]

As employees, caregivers are responsible for many babies close in age and confined to one place; they share their work with other nonrelated adult caregivers, and they are accountable (often subject to legal liability) to supervisors, parents, and often state licensing representatives. The idea that caregivers provide nurturance is contradicted by the simultaneous expectation that they be "professional"—understood as an emotionally neutral role (Power, 1987).[11] As Sheldon White (1983) wrote, caregivers, "denying that they should enter a child's emotional life . . . do not. (Or rather, they do so but in incalculable and not-so-positive ways)" (p. 12).

UNSURPASSABLE CHILDHOODS

The seriality of day care lies in the children's and caregivers' shared occupation of and confinement to the center. Despite the amount of time they are grouped together, the adults and children are emotionally isolated. Despite caregivers' sometimes physical overinvolvement with children, the emotional culture is impoverished. Throughout this text, the field notes reveal how caregivers fail to enter into these young children's lives, share their experiences, and see, understand, and respond to their emotional expressions and perspectives. The field notes throughout reveal a "plurality of isolations" (Sartre, 1960/1976, p. 256) where people do *not care* about or for each other.

"The ability to nurture oneself and to nurture others is developed through the experience of having been nurtured" (Love & Shanklin, 1983, p. 283). These children are being denied the experience of being nurtured. The emotional isolation and depersonalization described here is not acceptable for *child care*, where *care* is supposed to have operative emphasis. Regardless of the possibilities for unconditional love these babies may receive from their parents during non-day care hours, the consequences for children spending as much as ten hours each day with emotionally uninvolved (and physically overinvolved) caregivers may have far-reaching implications. As children's emotions, and their selves, are not given meaning through recognition and response, caregivers facilitate "the loss of being one's self" (Schroeder, 1984, p. 134) for each child.[12] Or, as Suransky (1983) concluded, "the child, to accommodate to the institution in which she is involuntarily placed, must allow the institution to strip her of the forms of childhood that constitute her child-self" (p. 154).

Shelby Steele's (1990) autobiographical account of teacher-inflicted punishment presents a more moving statement of the consequences for children's selves and

how one's innate capacity for insecurity is expanded and deep-
ened, of how a disbelieving part of the self is brought to life and
forever joined to the believing self. As children we are all
wounded in some way and to some degree by the wild world we
encounter. From these wounds a disbelieving *anti-self* is born, an
internal antagonist saboteur that embraces the world's negative
view of us, that believes our wounds are justified by our own un-
worthiness, and that entrenches itself as a lifelong voice of
doubt. (p. 36)

While children are active agents in their own constructions of the world, they come to understand themselves in the mir-
ror of what others have constructed as a world (Wartofsky, 1983).
As Sartre wrote, "through the Other's look I *live* myself"
(1943/1956, p. 359).[13] What is the "look" of the caregiver toward
the child? I contend, upon reflection and interpretation of the field
notes herein, that the look of the caregiver very often amounts to
the insignificance of the child in child care, as their intentionality
and emotionality are severely constrained in these child care centers. For these children, their participation in group care requires
the loss, or submersion of, individuated selfhood. The day care
group becomes Heidegger's crowd where children are "lulled into
inauthentic existence" (Schroeder, 1984, p. 129).

Wartofsky (1983) cautions us not to underestimate the extent to which children create, differentiate, and individuate themselves. Others point out that singular events may not be decisive
and deterministic of future development, as there is some evidence that later experiences ameliorate earlier ones (see Kagan,
1984; Yarrow, 1979). But at the same time, "the experiences and
feelings of childhood endure" (Bowman, 1989, p. 450); "every experience lives on in further experiences" (Dewey, 1938, p. 28).
Children "feel strongly, and recall those feelings from a very early
age. However, as young children they are as yet unable to speak
about them" (Piers, 1989, p. xiii). Thus our adult obligation to project ourselves empathetically into the world of the child and attempt to understand her language of gestures.

Repeated emotional experiences do affect emotional
practices and understandings (Denzin, 1984). These children's
emotional experiences are integrated into their understandings
about themselves, others, and the world they share. They become
part of their personal biography—and in these cases, their personal troubles. The particular ways children live the world of day
care may amount to an "unsurpassable childhood" (Sartre,

1960/1963, p. 65), as children attempt to make meaning and construct their worlds within a rigidly managed, impoverished emotional setting.

SUMMARY

In this chapter I have described problematic emotional interactions between the caregivers and the children. These situations illustrate how children and their caregivers are caught in Sartre's field of the practico-inert, a field where they are emotionally isolated, where children are objectified and where caregivers are alienated as they engage in emotional labor. I conclude with the suggestion that these epiphanic moments profoundly and negatively affect the meanings children assign to themselves, others, and their worlds.

5
Emotionally Responsive, Empowering Child Care

> If I am a consciousness turned toward things, I can meet in
> things the actions of another and find in them a meaning, be-
> cause they are themes of possible activity for my own body.
> —Merleau-Ponty, *The Primacy of Perception*

Sartre maintained that the alienation of seriality is not absolute; in the group it can be "transformed into a positive, internal reciprocity, a free cooperative association of mutual recognition" (Hirsch, 1982, p. 76). I believe this can occur with infants and toddlers and their caregivers in group day-care settings, although I have rarely observed it. Implicit in this critique of the problematic relations of power and emotion between children and their caregivers is a more positive image of caregiving. I believe babies should be held when they cry, allowed to sleep when tired, to be self-directed in play—in general, to be emotionally supported as they act on their own emerging initiative and pursue their "projects."

In this chapter I explore the concept of emotionally responsive, empowering caregiving within infant-toddler day care centers, and construct a picture for the reader of a "child-friendly" (Polakow, 1992) program. In this process I draw upon the same philosophical and theoretical perspectives applied in the interpretation of problematic experience in order to *imagine* the possibilities for emotionally responsive, empowering care. This involves the positing of philosophical assertions about children's development in the context of relationships, and the presentation of field notes to illustrate their meaning and implications. I conclude this chapter with some thoughts as to how center-based day care programs might be organized so as to support emotionally responsive, empowering caregiving.

THE CONCEPT OF
RESPONSIVE CAREGIVING

> Most vital . . . is that the infant or toddler is cared for in ways
> that promote his feeling effective, respected, and understood
> much of the time. The sense of having needs met—the sense
> that relationships hold promise . . . will develop within rela-
> tionships with others.
> —Pawl, "Infants in day care"

Responsive caregiving is the foundation for the young child's experience of freedom, of his or her sense of autonomy and empowerment. In turn, emotional engagement and emotional authenticity underlie responsive caregiving.[1] The child's self is known in the experience of connection and defined by the responsiveness of human engagement (see Gilligan, 1988). Thus, empowerment and emotionality are linked in responsive caregiving. As Packer wrote (1987), "the young child develops social agency and independence as a skillful social being as a consequence of being involved in deeply intimate exchanges" (pp. 3–4).

Responsive caregiving refers to the nature of the interactions between the child and the caregiver. It is a concept that goes beyond physical caretaking to include a sense of personal, emotional involvement that is mutual, or at least potentially so. Responsive caregiving requires respect for children as active, emotional subjects; reflection on the meanings of their language of gestures; and responsiveness to their efforts to communicate and pursue their project of being. The emotionally responsive caregiver attempts to enter and participate in the child's world, to understand and respond to her lived experience, including her emotional expressions and understandings. This is child care "grounded in the being of the child" (Suransky, 1977, p. 291).

Responsive caregiving for infants and toddlers in group settings is not simply a matter of technical skill or implementing a set of prescriptions for practice. There are no fixed and specific formulas (Gabarino, Stott, and the Faculty of The Erickson Institute, 1989; Noddings, 1992). In what follows, I explore three related facets of responsive caregiving: an understanding and appreciation of the child, reciprocity, and empathy. These are the themes that are absent from the field notes in chapters 3 and 4.

THE CHILD IN
CHILD CARE

> Toddlerhood represents the tension between two ever-present
> yet opposing human impulses: the exhilarating thrust of care-
> free, unrestricted, uninhibited exploration . . . and the longing
> to feel safe in the protective sphere of intimate relationships.
> —Lieberman, "Attachment and exploration"

Responsive caregiving requires a particular understanding and appreciation of the child. "Attachment, intimacy, empathy, separation, autonomy and sense of self and self-worth are
major issues in the first three years of life" (Pawl, 1990b, p. 7). Children are active, reflective, interpreting, emotional participants in
the day care environment. As Polakow (1992) wrote, children "are
in the world; they act upon the world; they discover things in the
world; and in so doing and acting, they are fulfilling a fundamental human activity of intentionality and purposiveness" (p. 173).
Consider the following scene described by Gonzalez-Mena and
Eyer (1993, pp. 68–69):

> *Three infants are lying on their backs, waving their arms,
> and looking around. A caregiver sits near them, rearranging brightly
> colored scarves to be within the reach of each child. A floppy beach
> ball is also available. One of the infants grabs it, waves it in the air,
> and lets it go. It lands near another of the infants, who regards it
> briefly, then turns back to gaze at the red scarf standing puffed up
> near his face.*

> *Beyond the small fenced-in area is a larger space where nine
> young toddlers are playing. Two are busily engaged in crawling in
> and out of the rungs of the ladder that is lying flat on the floor. One
> leaves to sit in an empty laundry basket nearby. He climbs out, turns
> it over, then crawls under it. He lifts it up to look out at two children
> who are trying on hats from a collection they have found in a box near
> a shelf of toys. One of these children puts three hats on his head, then
> picks up two in his hands and runs over to the fence and throws the
> hats, one by one, into the area where the infants are lying. He gig-
> gles delightedly at the reaction he gets from the surprised infants.
> The other hat player in the meantime has loaded several into the
> back of a small toddler trike and is riding around the room. He stops
> at a low table where several children are squeezing zip-lock bags full
> of different substances. He looks at the caregiver sitting there when
> she says to one of the squeezers, "You really like the soft one, don't*

you?" He briefly pokes one of the bags. Finding it interesting, he abandons the hats and the trike and sits down at the table to explore the other bags.

In another area of the room, a girl is hauling large plastic-covered foam blocks from one corner and piling them on the couch, which is pulled out a few feet from the wall. Then she climbs up on the couch and proceeds to throw the cushions over the back until she has nearly filled the space. She gets down, walks around, and jumps on the pile she has made.

In another part of the room, a child is sitting with a caregiver on a large mattress. . . . The two are "reading" a book together. They are joined by one of the bag squeezers, who plops down on the adult's lap and takes the book away. It is quickly replaced by the other child, who has a stack of books next to her on the mattress.

From a phenomenological perspective, childhood and the process of development can be seen as creating a home in the world (B. Vandenberg, 1987a; D. Vandenberg, 1971). "The child as a conscious *becoming* being pursues a 'project' of freedom in order to become someone-himself and not a being for others" (Polakow, 1992, p. 177). Child development, then, is not simply a straightforward, linear accumulation of skills, concepts, and competencies.

This view of the child suggests that child care is not simply a matter of technique, manipulation, and method, but a matter of *engagement*. Infants are communicators and social participants from birth. Their gestures, cries, vocalizations, and actions call out to their caregivers to understand and respond. As Pawl (1990b) noted, it is in the context of relationships that the needs and wishes of very young children are met—or not. It is in the context of relationships that infants and toddlers continue to develop expectations about how the world is, how the adults in that world behave, and their own place in the social world. Thus, caregivers have a crucial role in the child's construction of his or her understandings of self and others.

RECIPROCITY

Reciprocity implies give-and-take, a mutual negotiation of meaning and power.
— Lather, "Research as praxis"

Emotionally responsive caregivers "presuppose a certain reciprocity on the part of the child" (Schutz & Luckmann, 1973, p.

246). Caregiver-child interaction and involvement are mutual in the sense that there is an exchange—a back and forth of responding between the adult and the child. As Saarni (1989) wrote, "a dynamic sequence of reciprocal emotional responding occurs [when] we react to the others' expressive behavior, which, in turn, influences the subsequent emotional response from the other, and so forth" (p. 185). The emotionally responsive caregiver allows herself to become part of this "fluid dovetailing process" of social-emotional negotiation (Saarni, 1989, p. 185). The episodes below illustrate this theme. The first scene is adapted from Gonzalez-Mena and Eyer (1993, pp 76–77).

> Keis (three months) was lying on a blanket on the floor, crying. Busy preparing his bottle, the caregiver called to him, "I know you're hungry, I'm coming." The cries lessened as Keis listened to the caregiver's voice. But when she didn't come immediately after, the cries resumed, louder now. The caregiver, twisting the cap onto the bottle, approached Keis, "I'm sorry you had to wait." As Keis continued to cry, she added, "I know, I know. I'm going to pick you up now so you can have your bottle." As the caregiver bent to lift him up, Keis slowed his crying and held out his arms. The caregiver gently picked him up and carried him to a rocking chair where she sat holding him while he took his bottle. While he drank, Keis looked up intently at the caregiver's face. "That's better, isn't it?" cooed the caregiver. Keis's body relaxed; one of his hands grasped the caregiver's hair. "You were really hungry, weren't you?" When the bottle was empty, the caregiver gave Keis a hug and kissed his forehead. He smiled as he gazed at his caregiver.

> It was time for Lela's (nine months) medicinal treatment for chronic respiratory disease. The caregiver told Lela it was time for her medicine, sat in the rocking chair, and held Lela on her lap. The treatment lasted several minutes and involved holding a mask over the child's nose and mouth. The caregiver rocked back and forth, stroked Lela's hair, and talked to her in a soothing voice, "You're so pretty, Lela. This will help you feel better. I know you don't like this, but it will be over in a few minutes. Then you'll feel better." While the caregiver tended to Lela, Kara (ten months) sat staring wide-eyed at them. Her eyes shifted from the caregiver to Lela and her mask. Noticing this, the caregiver said to Kara, "It's okay, Kara. I'm helping Lela so that she can breathe better." While this went on, Todd (ten months) stood up in his crib and began to whimper. Although the caregiver had her hands full and could not get up, she called to Todd, "To-od, I'll be with you in a minute, hon. Lela needs her medicine right

now." Then she focused her attention on Lela again, "good girl, you're doing fine, we're almost finished." When the treatment was over, the caregiver gave Lela a little hug and put her down on the carpet, saying, "Now you'll feel better." She turned her attention to Todd. She picked him up out of his crib, sat down with him, Kara, and Lela on the floor with some toys, and played with them.

Lela's caregiver was able to involve herself with the feelings of more than one child—a challenge in group care. She acknowledged each child, offered explanation and comfort, and physically attended to them as she was able.

Understanding and responding to children as human beings (versus objects) relies considerably on the caregivers' abilities to observe and interpret children's language of gestures. As the situations below demonstrate, this is not always an easy task. The first scene is adapted from Reynolds (1990, p. 85).

Bonnie (fourteen weeks) was lying on her back on a pillow on the floor. Suddenly she began to squirm and whimper. The caregiver noticed her distress and knelt beside her. She checked Bonnie's diaper. It was dry. She looked at Bonnie's chart to see how recently she had eaten and decided she was probably not hungry. As she checked everything, the caregiver carried on a conversation with Bonnie, "Are you wet? Maybe you're hungry. Yes, I can see you're upset. Let's see what I can do to make you happy." Thinking Bonnie might want a change of position, the caregiver turned her over onto her tummy. Bonnie began to cry loudly. Still talking to Bonnie, the caregiver turned her on her back again. She noticed that Bonnie kept looking up intently. The caregiver realized that Bonnie had been watching and listening to a musical mobile hanging above her. The mobile had stopped moving and playing, unnoticed by the caregiver. The caregiver said, "Oh, Bonnie, would you like me to wind the mobile?" as she wound the mobile. Bonnie, watching her, relaxed, sighed, and followed the mobile with her eyes again. She seemed satisfied.

Amber (ten months) was sitting in the high chair and did not appear happy. The caregiver was trying to feed her, offering different choices to find one that Amber would eat. Amber refused everything. The caregiver talked to her, "What's wrong, Amber? Aren't you hungry today?" Amber started to cry and throw food off her tray. The caregiver finally said, "Okay, Amber, I'll pick you up, is that what you want?" As the caregiver picked her up, Amber's crying slowed, and then stopped. She put her arms around the caregiver's neck and her head on her shoulder. The caregiver rubbed Amber's back and talked to her softly.

The caregiver finished feeding Molly (seven months) her lunch. She wiped Molly's face and hands, picked her up, and sat her down on the carpet. Molly frowned, began to cry, and lifted her arms straight up into the air. The caregiver looked at her and said, "What's the matter, Molly? Don't you want to be on the floor?" She picked Molly up and put her into the walker. Again Molly cried a little and reached her arms up. This time, instead of picking Molly up, the caregiver put some toys on the tray of the walker, selecting one to shake to attract Molly's interest. Molly stopped crying and reached for the toy.

The caregivers above made the effort to consider how the world seemed to appear and feel to these infants. Moreover, they *respected*, rather than discounted or denied, the children's experiences and feelings, as they responded with interest, flexibility, and sensitivity.

EMPATHY

> Caring involves stepping out of one's own personal frame of reference into the other's. When we care, we consider the other's point of view, his objective needs, and what he expects of us. Our attention, our mental engrossment is on the cared-for, not on ourselves. . . .
>
> —Noddings, *Caring*

The situations thus far described in this chapter illustrate another theme of emotionally responsive, empowering caregiving: empathy for the child's feelings and situation. Empathic understanding depends upon, and at the same time allows for, adult-child communication, that is, the reciprocal emotional responding described above. The empathic capacity involves connecting one's own experience to that of others, and through that connection, gaining understanding of their feelings. Denzin (1984) has described this as emotional intersubjectivity and emotional embracement. "The subjective interpretation of another's emotional experience from one's own standpoint is central to emotional understanding" (Denzin, 1984, p. 137). Caregivers merely have to imagine the realness of the children's experiences for themselves, to consider how things might look and feel to the child.[2] Scheler (1913/1970) described this as "fellow-feeling" (pp. 13–14):

> Fellow-feeling involves an intentional reference to the feelings of another and is felt simply as a feeling-for-him. In fellow-feeling there is a reaction to the state and value of the other's feelings— as these are visualized in vicarious feeling. (Denzin, 1984, p. 148)

Consider the following field notes.

> *Avon (eight weeks) needed his diaper changed. Once on the changing table he began to cry. The caregiver explained he needed his diaper changed, but Avon persisted in his crying. The caregiver tried again to calm him by telling him he was dirty and that she was going to change him and make him feel comfortable again. Avon continued to cry hard. The caregiver then stopped the diaper changing process and rubbed Avon's tummy in an attempt to soothe him. In a soothing tone she told Avon there was no need to be upset or afraid, she only wanted to make him more comfortable. As Avon calmed, the caregiver told him she needed to take off his clothes because they were wet. She proceeded to do this, then cleaned him up and put a fresh diaper and clothes on. All the while she continued to talk soothingly to Avon, with comments such as, "I think you're all clean now," and "Gee, I hope these pj's fit you." By the time she had finished, Avon was a clean, happy baby again.*

Although this infant was only eight weeks old, the caregiver seemed to regard him as an individual with feelings. Avon was more than a body to be changed (in contrast to the situation with Lena described in chapter 4, p. 52). The caregiver attempted to view the experience from the child's perspective and accordingly reassured him. The routine, while necessary, was secondary to the child's experience of it—indeed, the caregiver stopped the routine momentarily to attend to the child.

Gilligan and Wiggins (1988) make a distinction between empathy and "co-feeling" that is applicable to the child-caregiver relationship:

> empathy implies an identity of feelings—that self and other feel the same, while co-feeling implies that one can experience feelings that are different from one's own. Co- feeling, then, depends on the ability to participate in another's feelings (in their terms),

signifying an attitude of judgement or observation. To feel with another any emotion means in essence to be *with* that person, rather than to stand apart and look *at* the other, feeling sympathy *for* her or him. . . . Co-feeling underlies respect for the feelings of others whether or not their needs are real. (pp. 122, 132)

The meaning and significance of this concept is illustrated by reconsidering a situation described in chapter 3:

It was snack time and all the children were directed to stop playing and sit at the table. Maggie (fourteen months) pushed her food away and began to cry. The caregiver said perhaps Maggie was tired and removed her from the table to change her diaper and then sat down to hold and rock her. Maggie squirmed in her arms, refusing to sit still. The caregiver let her down on the floor where she played contentedly. Observing this, the caregiver said to the other adults, "Next time Maggie must sit through snack time. She wasn't tired, she just wanted to play."

To the above caregiver, Maggie's feelings weren't "real," or legitimate, thus they weren't deserving of an accommodating response. But if the caregiver's actions were instead guided by co-feeling, the "realness" would have been irrelevant. The observation that Maggie did not want a snack and wished instead to play might have been respected. In a more responsive setting the field notes might have been reconstructed as follows:

The toddlers were at play at various places in the room. Snack was brought in and set on the table. About half the children immediately ran to the table, while the others continued to play. The caregiver helped them to wash up, sit down, and serve themselves. A few more children joined them. The caregiver asked Maggie, still at play, if she would like a snack. Maggie said "no," and continued to play. Meanwhile, Hannah got down from her chair to return to play. About fifteen minutes later, Maggie indicated she was ready for a snack and approached the table. The caregiver assisted her.

In the above reconstruction, the situation was structured to minimize conflict and power struggles. Instead of much of their energy going to managing children, the adults were free to become involved with them and supportive of their activity. Moreover, the routine was managed with respect for the inclinations of individual children.

IMAGES OF
EMOTIONALLY RESPONSIVE,
EMPOWERING CAREGIVING

> Caring is both who you are and what you do.
> —Oakley, *Feminism, motherhood, and medicine*

Polakow (1992) conceptualized "an authentic existential landscape" as one which permits the child to experience the "dialectic of structure and freedom" (p. 184). As the situation below demonstrates, a young child's empowerment does not depend upon a romantic notion of noninterference (another kind of neglect and disengagement). Neither is it an unyielding child centeredness which sacrifices the self of the caregiver or other children.

> *Avery (two years) came out from the washroom to find Calvin seated at the snack table with the caregiver. The other three chairs at the table were empty. Avery grabbed the back of Calvin's chair. "That's my seat!" he said angrily. Calvin did not respond. "Calvin is sitting there today," explained the caregiver. Avery emphatically repeated, "He's in my spot!" The caregiver suggested that Avery sit in a different chair today. With a great show of resignation Avery found a different chair. As he sat down, the caregiver said to him, "You like that spot, don't you?" referring to the disputed territory. "Uh-huh," Avery replied. "Maybe you can sit there tomorrow," suggested the caregiver. "Okay," Avery responded happily, and proceeded to eat his snack.*

In this situation Avery looked to the caregiver to settle a dispute and advocate on his behalf. The caregiver went beyond an intervention that simply redirected Avery to acknowledging his feelings. She may have understood that Avery's distress and attempt to remove Calvin derived from a need for constancy and order, and a sense of possessiveness and ritual typical of many two-year-olds. At any rate, Avery perceived Calvin's place as his and the displacement upset him. The caregiver allowed Avery to verbally express his feelings, and permitted him a degree of autonomy in selecting another chair. No rules were invoked, nor was physical control necessary.

> To care is to act not by fixed rule but by affection and regard . . . to act as one caring, then, is to act with special regard for the particular person in a concrete situation. (Noddings, 1984, p. 24)

In responsive caregiving, as each child is appreciated for him- or herself, caregivers make a conscious decision to attend to the particular child and the particular situation. This often requires treating some children differently from others, for example, holding them longer or more often, or excusing them from scheduled routines. Yet all the children are still equally cared for, according to their differences. Caregiving, understood this way, requires and allows caregivers the flexibilty to look at and respond to children as individuals without feeling they are unfairly making exceptions.

The episode below demonstrates how simple and satisfactory flexibility and responsiveness can be, as a caregiver, recognizing, understanding, and empathizing with a child, allowed his needs to have primacy over the schedule. Children's empowerment develops out of this recognition, and the growing sense that their feelings and actions have meaning to those adults who care for them.

It was lunchtime and all the toddlers were starting to eat, except Misha who was sitting in his chair not eating. The practicum student tried, unsuccessfully, to find out what was wrong. The caregiver sat near Misha, expressed her concern, and offered to hold him. Realizing he was sleepy, the caregiver helped him to lie down on his cot. A little while later, on his own initiative, he came back to the table. He seemed to feel better and finished eating his lunch.

When caregivers attend to the child and the child's experience of lived time, then the *process* of managing daily routines and activities becomes as important as accomplishing them. A daily schedule in itself isn't necessarily oppressive. Indeed, routine is often a source of continuity and security, provided the desire for efficient management doesn't take precedence over the intentionality, development, and emotional and physical needs of the children. A responsive daily schedule is one that serves as a provisional, not an absolute, guide—a supportive framework for action which is open to possibilities for spontaneity and flexibility. I have described this elsewhere as "following the child's lead" (Leavitt & Eheart, 1985). This requires flexibility, and a willingness to give up some control to the child. If we look to the child, attempt to see the world from the child's perspective, and allow the child the "freedom to create and construct" (Freire, 1970, p. 55), *sharing* power with children, it is possible to humanize the child care center.

In the following pages I present additional field notes illustrative of emotionally responsive, empowering child care.

Arrival

When I arrived some children were already involved in play with a caregiver. Another caregiver "floated." As individual children arrived with their parents, this "floater" moved to the entrance to greet them. "Good morning, Patty!" Patty (nineteen months) was new to the center. The caregiver knelt down to touch her shoulder and look into her face. "Let me help you with your buttons, then you can take your coat and hang it in your 'cubby'." Once Patty's coat was put away, the caregiver took her on a tour of the room, her mother following. "Let's see what there is to play with today. We have 'Legos' over here, there's blocks and playdough. . . ." Patty ran over to the library corner, selected a book and climbed onto the sofa to look at it. Her mother followed, and seeing that she was settled said, "Bye-bye, Patty. See you later." Patty looked up at her mother and said "No!" The caregiver said, "I'll stay with you, Patty, and read you the story, okay?" Patty sadly watched her mother go and then turned her attention to the caregiver, who gave her a brief hug, saying, "It's hard to say goodbye, I know." She asked Patty if she would like to sit on her lap, and Patty nodded "yes." They sat on the sofa together to look at the book Patty had selected. The other caregiver, aware of the situation, took over the "floater" role for a while.

Play

The caregiver took Jeannie (thirteen months) out of the high chair and put her on the carpet. The caregiver then went to put a cassette in the tape player. Meanwhile Jeannie stood up and looked around the room. She looked up and said "Hi" to a parent entering the room. When the parent returned the "Hi," Jeannie smiled. About that time the music started to play. Jeannie began to clap her hands and rock her head sideways. The caregiver said to her, "Are you dancing?" and began rocking her head in imitation of Jeannie. Jeannie smiled and laughed and rocked her entire body. When the song ended, both the caregiver and Jeannie clapped their hands and said, "Yea!" Jeannie looked around the room for a minute and then walked over to another caregiver and tapped her on the leg a few times, and waited for the caregiver to turn around and notice her. She did, and smiled at Jeannie, who raised her arms in the air above her head. "Do you want to dance with me?" the caregiver asked as she picked up Jeannie. Jeannie smiled and laughed some more, and danced in the caregiver's arms.

Diapering

The caregiver lifted Leroy (thirteen months) out of his crib saying to him, "Leroy, you need a clean diaper." Once on the changing table Leroy squirmed and kicked his legs. "I'm sorry, Leroy, I can see you don't want to be changed, but you'll just have to put up with this for a minute," the caregiver said sympathetically. "First we have to get your jeans off," she said as she struggled to pull them down over his diaper. As Leroy squirmed and tried to turn over she said, "I know, you really don't like this. You'd rather be playing." She continued undressing him and unfastened his diaper. Leroy tried to sit up. She held him down firmly, "I know you want to get up. In a minute. Here, you can help by holding the 'Desitin,'" she said as she handed the tube to him, which he grasped. "Okay, now I can wipe you clean. Here is a nice fresh diaper. Doesn't that feel good? Almost finished. There, all done!" "Down!" demanded Leroy. "Yes, I'll put you down now," the caregiver said, holding out her arms as Leroy sat up and leaned into her. She put Leroy on the floor and he ran over to a canister of colored plastic shapes which he happily dumped onto the floor.[3]

Play

The toddlers were finishing their snack. One by one their faces were wiped clean by the caregivers and they were directed to the carpet to play. The process took about twenty minutes. In the meantime, the children who had finished were left unattended, although still close by. They played happily, pulling out all the toys within their reach: rubber balls, little toy people and houses, riding toys, and dolls. There was also a climbing structure at one end of the room which the children were gleefully all over, carrying their toys with them as they climbed up and crawled down the slide. The caregivers, finished with the children, moved on to clean the tables and floor at a leisurely pace, occassionally glancing toward the children. Cleanup took another ten minutes, during which the children continued to play purposefully, happily, and without conflict.

Lunch

Jon had spilled his milk at the lunch table and the caregiver told him to get a paper towel and clean it up. As Jon went to do this, Ted also rose from the table and began walking to the paper towel dispenser. The caregiver said, "Ted, you don't need to be up, please sit down." Ted kept walking, so the caregiver got up and took his hand and led him back to his seat. He sat there, silent, and did not resume eating his lunch; he looked angry. Noticing his expression, the caregiver said, "You're angry because I made you sit down." She paused and asked, "Why were you up anyway?" Ted did not answer, so I said, "I think Ted wanted to help clean up Jon's spill." The caregiver replied, "Oh, he probably did." She turned to Ted and said, "Is that right, Ted? I'm sorry. Next time I'll try to pay more attention."

Nap Time

The caregiver put on a record of classical music to play softly as the toddlers prepared for their naps. Patty was lying on her cot, crying for her mother. The caregiver approached her, knelt down, put her hand on Patty's shoulder and said, "You must be very upset and missing your mom." Patty continued to sob. The caregiver added, "It must be scary to sleep in a new place." Patty cried some more. "Maybe it will help if I pat your back," offered the caregiver. She gently rubbed Patty's back. After a while Patty's sobbing subsided and she fell asleep.[4]

Transition from
Nap to Snack

The toddlers were beginning to awaken from their naps. The caregivers left the lights off as they approached individual children to change their diapers and dress them. Patty sat up on her cot and rubbed her eyes as the caregiver picked her up. "Did you sleep well, Patty? Let's get you into a dry diaper," she said in a quiet voice. Other children continued to sleep while Patty and a few other toddlers were dressed. Once dressed, these toddlers were directed to a corner of the room where they could choose to play quietly with puzzles or look at books. The caregiver opened the curtain so some light came in on them through the window. Meanwhile, the other caregiver had been attending to other children as they gradually woke up. After about one-half hour all but one child was up and dressed and playing. The *caregivers put the day's snack onto two tables: a basket of graham crackers and a small pitcher of juice. Patty helped the caregiver set out napkins and plastic cups at each place. Noticing this activity, the toddlers who had been playing quietly approached the table and began climbing into their chairs, with the caregivers' help. Each child was given a wet, warm washcloth to clean their hands and faces. After they were collected, one caregiver sat at each table and passed the basket of crackers around so that each toddler could help him or herself. "Would you like a cracker, Patty? Who's thirsty?" the caregiver asked as she poured juice into cups. "Me!" piped up several toddlers. Patty noticed that Jody was still sleeping and asked the caregiver, "What about Jody?" The caregiver replied, "I guess she's extra sleepy today. We'll save some juice and crackers for her to have later." Satisfied, Patty nibbled at her cracker. The caregivers talked with the children, reviewing the morning's activities and describing the planned afternoon walk to the park.*

Transition from
Snack to Play

Two of the toddlers finished their snack and, on their own initiative, rose from the table. The caregiver had placed some carpet squares on the floor and told the children to sit on them in preparation for "group time." They were encouraged to look at some books while they waited. As more children finished with their snack, they also were directed to move to a carpet square with a book of their choice. Eventually all the children were on their squares looking at books. By the time the caregiver had cleaned up the tables, some of the children were beginning to drift away from the group into other play areas. The caregiver noticed this and decided to skip group time and allow the children to continue to play with materials of their choice.

Play

Today some men were working on the road in front of the day-care center. They were using a jackhammer. The children (two-year-olds) were playing inside at the time and heard the noise through some open windows. Several children ran to the windows to see what was going on. They climbed on shelves and chairs in order to see. The caregivers tried to to get them down, saying they didn't want the children to get hurt, but the children kept climbing back up.

Finally, the caregivers decided that the children could go outside to watch the workmen. After about ten minutes of watching the workmen, some children decided they would like to play on the slide. One caregiver supervised these children and the other stayed with those still interested in the jackhammer. The planned activity, collage-making, was abandoned until later.

Late Afternoon

It was about 5:00 P.M. Just three toddlers were still in the room. Hannah and James had pulled a bin full of plastic farm animals off the shelves and were playing with them on the carpet. They asked the caregiver if they could have the barns and other accessory farm toys to play with. These toys were in another room, but the caregiver agreed, and returned with two barns which she set on the carpet for Hannah and James. Patty, observing this, said she wanted a barn, too. Hearing Patty, Hannah started to whimper and said, "My farm!" (She seemed to think she would be required to share.) James became upset then, too. The caregiver said, "I think there might be one for each of you. Would you like to help me look, Patty?" This action seemed to instantly calm all three children. The caregiver took Patty's hand and they went to find another barn. Hannah was left with her barn, to which she turned her attention in play.

Spencer Cahill (1990) explains the significance of these seemingly simple and all too often taken-for-granted experiences described in the field notes presented here.

> The tired child who is laid to rest or the crying child who is comforted begins to realize that she is not alone with her private experiences. She begins to realize that they are expressed to others and can be shared with them. Here is the cornerstone of that social structuring of experience that we call the "self." (p. 2)

This self is an empowered self.[5] Its basis is in self-affirmation, emotional authenticity and security, and the boundaries of protection provided by the caregivers. When caregivers emotionally embrace children, each child is conceptualized and felt as a valued other. In this process, children's emotional selves are recognized, validated, taken into account, and allowed expression—they are given voice and empowered. It is in relation to the child's *emotions*, as well as intentionality, that the caregiver can give freedom (see Bergmann, 1977). This is lived freedom, not an intellectual or political abstraction, but rooted in the lived situation (Morrison, 1988). In Gilligan's (1988) words, for the child in responsive care,

> being dependent, then, no longer means being helpless, powerless, and without control; rather it signifies a conviction that one is able to have an effect on others, as well as the recognition that the interdependence of attachment empowers both the self and the other, not one person at the other's expense. The activities of care—being there, listening, the willingness to help, and the ability to understand—take on a moral dimension, reflecting the injunction to pay attention and not to turn away from need. (p. 16)

THE CENTER AS A SETTING FOR RESPONSIVE CARE

> The experience of caring and being cared for is intimately bound up with the way we define ourselves and our social relations.
> —Graham, Caring: A labour of love

The themes of responsive caregiving presented here —reciprocity, empathy, and respect for the individual child—are not new to the literature on child rearing. There is much we understand at this time about how children develop their competencies and self-understandings in the context of social relationships.[6] There are some excellent texts on infant-toddler caregiving in day care centers that elaborate the practical dimensions of daily caregiving (e.g., Gonzalez-Mena & Eyer, 1993; Leavitt & Eheart, 1985; Reynolds, 1990; Willis & Ricciuti, 1975). What meanings caregivers bring to and derive from these texts, if they read them, is another issue. There are few model programs to which they can turn to understand the meanings of responsive caregiving in practice (Whitebook, Howes, & Phillips, 1989). This problem is compounded by the inadequacy of both "mothering" and "schooling" as sufficient models for the unique setting of infant-toddler day care.

The field notes in this chapter demonstrate that it is certainly possible for caregivers to become more child-aware, and more reflective in their everday practices, and consequently more responsive within their existing settings. The question emerges as to why caregivers so often appear so unable to meet these children in their worlds. It is necessary to go beyond a critique of the individual caregiver, and examine how the organizational and administrative structure of the day-care center supports or constrains the development of reciprocal emotional relationships between adults and children.

Temporal and Spatial
Dimensions of Care

It is reasonable to suggest that apprehension and appreciation of, and feeling for, the child is enhanced by an ongoing, long-term emotional relationship, a shared history. This possibility is limited for caregivers by the temporal dimensions of their task and the numbers of children involved. For example, in some of the centers described here, children have been in as many as four or more different classroom groups by the time they are two years old. Assigned to rooms according to their ages, they typically progress from Infant I (six weeks to twelve months) to Infant II (twelve to eighteen months) to Toddler I (eighteen to twenty-four months) to Toddler II or the Two-year-old Room. These minute divisions emphasizing ordering and categorizing are primarily for management purposes. The erroneous assumption is the narrower the category (in this case, age), the more similar and homogeneous are children's needs and routines, and the more efficiently they can be managed. The economic influence is apparent as well: the highest demand is for infant care. The quicker infants are moved "up," the sooner room is made for new infants, providing additional income for centers. Again, the commercialization of care, even in nonprofit centers, exerts its influence.

In addition to being "promoted" from room to room, during the time they spend in each of these subdivisions, each child typically is cared for by a minimum of four different adults each day. Cost-effective efforts to maximize mandated group size allowances and meet staff-child ratios usually require at least two adults for every group of children at any one time. Moreover, staffing day care programs open for ten to twelve hours usually means that a child spending the whole day will not have been greeted at the beginning of the day by the same person who says goodbye (Calder, 1985). By the time a child is two years old, if enrolled since infancy, this child has been "cared for" by a *minimum* of sixteen adults in four different settings (substitutes and staff turnover increase this minimum). These factors make it extremely difficult for both the children and their caregivers to establish and maintain reciprocal emotional relationships.

These observations suggest that we reconsider how children are grouped, and how these groups are staffed, in day-care programs. For example, centers might still have four rooms for infants and toddlers, but children, instead of "graduating" every six to twelve months, might stay in one room with the same caregivers for an extended period of time, up to two or three years of age, adjusting the physical environment as necessary.[7] New children might be enrolled in any one of similarly age grouped rooms, as families leave through natural attrition and as children move on to preschool age (three to five years) groups (if desired).

Consider also the caregivers' workday, as it is affected by the larger conception of the workday/week in society at large: "a daily work rhythm fixed by profit-making rather than by the construction of humane work schedules" (Harvey, 1989, p. 231). This workday exerts control over the temporal context of the personal experiences of the caregivers and children. Given the demands and intensity of entering the child's world, should caregivers work eight hours each day with children? In many programs, caregivers do not get legally mandated breaks, because the demands of the children are too constant or because centers are insufficiently staffed to maintain mandated staff-child ratios while caregivers break.

In their study of staff burnout and working conditions, Maslach and Pines (1977) noted that the more hours caregivers worked directly with children, the more they experienced stress and revealed negative attitudes. They became rigid in managing routines, for example, insisting all children take compulsory naps. As caregivers apply procedures without variation regardless of situation or individual, they "fail to be present in their interactions" with the children; "caring disappears and only its illusion remains" (Noddings, 1984, p. 26). These observations suggest that the number of hours caregivers work in direct contact with children be reduced, perhaps to six each day. The other two hours of a full workday (as currently defined) might be spent in administrative tasks (for example, keeping developmental records), communicating with parents, and in inservice education and professional development of a kind which renews and expands caregivers' commitment and capacities for responsive care. I now turn to a discussion of what this inservice might entail.

Caring for
Caregivers

The caregiver is the very center of the young child's experience in day care; "we do not need hundreds of studies to know that a positive relationship between a child and caregiver is essential" (Zigler & Lang, 1991, pp. 65–66). Nonetheless, as a society we have failed to recognize the critical importance and demanding challenges of the caregivers' task. We cannot assume that, because they are women,[8] caregivers will have some "natural" empathy and the requisite skills to care for a group of very young children not their own.

The demands of responsive caregiving create very high expectations for caregivers. In exploring the meaning of responsive caregiving, as I have done here, it is easy to echo the romantic descriptions of mothering found in the Rousseaun tradition, where total immersion and patient devotion and sacrifice were part of the duties and glory of mothering (see Block & Block, 1980; Elshtain, 1981). Total selflessness on the part of the caregiver may actually impede her ability to care, as she loses *her self* in the process. One challenge presented for caregivers, then, centers on their ability to maintain their own sense of well-being, while caring for the children (see Gilligan, 1982). As Hochschild (1983) described it, the challenge of emotional labor is adjusting oneself to the role of caregiver in such a way that "allows some flow of self into the role but minimizes the stress the role puts on the self" (p. 188).

Despite an emerging body of literature on the professionalization of caregivers and the administration of child care programs, the caregivers' need to be cared for in order to develop and demonstrate their capacities for emotionally responsive caregiving is largely unaddressed. Foucault (1988) suggested that the domination of others and the exercise of tyrannical power derives from one's lack of care for oneself. As Noddings (1984) pointed out, if we fail to support and care for the caregiver, "she may be entirely lost as one-caring. If caring is to be maintained, clearly, the one-caring must be maintained" (p. 100).

In a program that supports caregivers' capacities for responsive caregiving, caregivers themselves are included in the compass of care. One dimension of this compass includes the opportunity and encouragement to become hermeneutic researchers, to explore how they live their lives in interplay with others—those children for whom they care, and those adults with whom they share this responsibility (Misgeld & Jardine, 1989). This concept parallels feminist consciousness-raising and critical pedagogy's dialogic encounter, processes by which individuals confront and explore their understandings of their experiences, particularly their daily problematics, and in so doing become capable of transforming their experience.[9]

Adults create emotionally stressful experiences for children perhaps because they do not remember their own childhood past. By remembering their own needs and vulnerabilities during childhood, caregivers may learn to recognize and respond to those of children (Bowman, 1989). Exploring the meanings of responsive caregiving for caregivers then becomes an "intensely personal affair" (Giroux, 1981, p. 158) as caregivers delve into their own childhoods, their own biographies. For caregivers, then, inquiry into the meaning of responsive caregiving is a process of self-inquiry and reflection, as well as self-care.[10]

Caregivers must become more self-aware, as well as child aware, and comfortable with their own and the children's emotionality. Caring for others and oneself involves "an awareness of oneself as capable of knowing and living with the feelings of others, as able to affect others and be affected by them" (Gilligan & Wiggins, 1988, p. 123). Self-awareness and self-care also require self-acceptance on the part of the caregiver:

> To feel for others (as distinguished from going through the motions of *doing* for others), to *feel with* others . . . , it is essential that the [caregiver] draw upon his [sic] own own capacity for feeling. And he can only do this if he respects his feelings and is at home with them, if he accepts them as part of himself. This means self-acceptance, which involves compassion for oneself. (Jersild, 1955, p. 133)

SUMMARY

In this chapter I have offered my construction of emotionally responsive, empowering caregiving. I have highlighted the importance of understanding the child as an active, reflective, communicative emotional being. I have posited the importance of reciprocity and empathy in responding to children in ways that support their personal empowerment, and I presented field notes to illustrate the meanings of these concepts. I also have offered suggestions as to how we might better tend to both caregivers and children in terms of the structure and organization of day-care centers. Finally, I suggested that caregiving is an activity requiring self-reflection on the part of the caregiver.

6
Infant-Toddler Day Care: Review, Reflections, and Directions

I am not a spectator, I am involved.
    —Merleau-Ponty, *The Phenomenology of Perception*

The aim of this project—to describe problematic lived experiences related to power and emotion of infants, toddlers, and their caregivers in day care centers—has involved a threefold purpose. First, my goal has been to bring these experiences and my interpretations of them before the reader. Second, this critique requires an exploration of the meanings of emotionally responsive, empowering caregiving within group care settings. These first two purposes involved a third: the attempt to integrate diverse philosophical perspectives to demonstrate the power of a multi-theoretical approach in the description and interpretation of lived experience. In this last chapter, I review the observations and understandings I have presented throughout this text related. to these three purposes, and offer some further reflections and directions.

REVIEW

Problematic Experience: Power

In the major portion of this text I have taken a close and critical look at children's and caregivers' shared occupation of and confinement to the day care center. I described the spatial regime which constrains children's actions and choices and subjects them to constant surveillance. The discussion of disciplinary control revealed another aspect of caregivers' control and exercise of extractive power over the children, particularly in the inflexible management of daily routines. Field notes illustrate how the caregivers' power also intrudes upon children's freedom to play. I have described the ways in which day care centers are constructed as sites of struggle, places where children's efforts to resist the caregivers' negative power and act with some autonomy are undermined. The caregivers' exercise of extractive power has been contrasted with the concept of transformative, developmental power, and emotionally responsive, empowering caregiving. I have shown how children's place in the social world of day care is to be docile and accepting of the caregivers' power, control, and unyielding authority.

Problematic
Experience: Emotion

The exercise of power occurs within an impoverished emotional setting. Children are objectified as they are physically managed by the caregivers, and as their emotional expressions and pleas are ignored, rejected, and denied. I have described the absence of reciprocity and empathy as caregivers go through the motions of "caring for" children. This emotional estrangement has been discussed in terms of alienated emotional labor—caring activity sold for a wage. That caregivers confront children and their work with hostility and resentment is an indication of how the work of caregiving is alienated labor. In essence, the description of the emotional culture of these day-care programs indicates the insignificance of the child and the *absence of care*. I express considerable concern for the particular ways children experience the world of day care, as they live through these epiphanic moments.

Emotionally Responsive,
Empowering Child Care

This description of the problematics of infant day care is not a call for a return to the mythical days when mothers stayed home and competently cared for their children.[1] Rather, it is a plea to revise exisiting social structures so that emotionally responsive, empowering caregiving might flourish in group child care settings. This is the rationale for the presentation in chapter 5. In these pages I explored the concepts involved in responsive caregiving: recognition of the child's intentionality and emotionality, responding to the child's language of gestures and engaging in reciprocal interactions, and responding with empathy to the child's emotional expressions and project of being. My plea to caregivers is that they recognize the importance of intersubjectivity, emotionality, particularity, and entering the world of the other as they engage in their caregiving task.

Given the demands of emotionally responsive caregiving, I also suggest that day care centers need to be reorganized in terms of grouping children, and the hours caregivers work with children, in order to attend to some of the temporal and spatial aspects of caregiving. Finally, I point to the need to care for the caregiver, and for caregiving to become a self-reflective activity. This requires caregivers to take their own emotionality seriously, and to become aware of the power they yield and its effects on the children in their care.

REFLECTIONS

> No ethic, and certainly no ethic of nurturance can be realized without a supporting politic.
> —Kuykendall, Toward an ethic of nurturance

Many of the problematics of caring within day-care centers emerge from conflicting cultural values long embedded within our society. Day-care programs, like schools, are likely to reflect and reify the values held explicitly or implicitly in our society. These values include our ideas about efficiency, control and objectivity, the public and private realms, the role of women in our society, and the place of children in our culture. These beliefs and values, and their saturation into our collective practices and routines, have developed historically. We cannot make significant changes in child care without such recognition.

The experience of children in programs organized in accord with an ideology of discipline and authority is not new. What *is* new is the increasing number of our youngest children—infants and toddlers—in group care programs for a significant number of hours each day, subjected to the same disciplinary control found in schools, factories, prisons, and other institutions. The discipline of standardized group care "is yet another expression and further extension of the scientifically inspired and rationalistic discipline of the modern age" (Cahill & Loseke, 1990, pp. 31, iii).

In a culture in which technical knowledge is highly valued, the relations between adults and children easily beome perceived as primarily a technical problem requiring a technical solution (Misgeld & Jardine, 1989). This phenomenon is intricately tied to

the power relations manifested in group care settings, most particularly in the management of children's time. Indeed, Misgeld
and Jardine suggest that a technical approach gains its predomi-
nance because it is a method of domination, a method relying on
control and manipulation.[2]

Some of the problematics of infant-toddler day care also
can be traced to our historical attitude toward out-of-home care
since the social construction of motherhood.[3] We have traditionally viewed substitute care arrangements as inherently inferior to
home rearing and mother care. This view is reinforced as it is constructed as a self-fulfilling prophecy when we fail to provide the
political, social, and economic supports responsive care demands.

The system of child care that has evolved has been in response, historically, to national crises, currents of social reform,
and society's economic needs.[4] As Fraser (1989) wrote, "the politics of day care has been a struggle to shape hegemonic understanding" in the struggle over "needs" (p. 173). All of these "needs"
(e.g., welfare reform) tend to ignore the caregiver and the children
in her care. To a great extent, these two groups—their experiences
and "needs"—are left out of the public policy discourse, despite the
often expressed view that children are "our most precious re-
source, our investment in the future."[5]

Some of the problematics of caregiving also emerge as it
has been historically constructed as a gendered task.

> Women are given caring work on the grounds that they are
> mothers, or may become mothers, or should have been mothers.
> They are even expected to *feel* like mothers while they work as
> [caregivers] . . . and to be satisfied with low pay or no pay. (New
> & David, 1985, p. 13)

Expecting the child care environment, as also a work environment, to reflect values and practices which run contrary to
those of, and lack credence in, the workplace (Leach & Page,
1987) presents a challenge for the most well-intentioned caregivers. Fraser (1989) notes the "conceptual dissonance" (p. 125)
between the roles of child rearer and worker, as these roles are
constituted as fundamentally incompatible with each other. The
role of the worker is a masculine role; the child-rearer role is
patently a feminine role. The private (feminine) realm ideals of
love, nurturance, and devotion are contrary to the "masculine" or
"scientific" ideals of the workplace which tend to emphasize routines, order, uniformity, rules, and procedures (Cann, 1987;

Kanter, 1975). And so, caregivers are confronted with a confused merger of realms where the boundaries for understanding and behavior are not at all clearly drawn; they may be unprepared for their conflicting roles and responsibilities in the situations in which they find themselves.

This project, then, in examining the problematic experiences of children and their caregivers, poses the question of what we can reasonably expect of caregivers in day-care centers. Children and their caregivers are not isolated in a self-contained unit of interaction; their joint problematic experience is reflective of political and social realities that go beyond the day-care center, permeating every sphere of our social existence. As we continue to place our youngest children in group care settings, it is important to consider under what conditions caring relations, emotional responsiveness, and children's developing autonomy can be sustained in these particular situations. Emotionally responsive, empowering caregiving requires attention to feeling, involvement, connection, compassion, respect, comfort, and nurturance—realms of experience neglected in our culture. Consequently, the endeavor to humanize the child care setting may depend upon fundamental changes in our beliefs and commitments. At the least, attention to the meanings in the phrase *child care* is a call for what Noddings described as an existentialist "awareness of and commitment to what we are doing" (1984, p. 35), as children's daily lived experiences and their own capacities to care are at stake here.

DIRECTIONS

Theoretical and
Philosophical Groundings

The review of the prevailing research on infant day care in chapter 1 points to the need for more self-conscious critiques of our research endeavors as well as projects which attend more explicitly to lived experience, interaction, and emotion. The field of early child care and education would benefit from a more interdisciplinary, multitheoretical approach in the study of children, and particularly their lived experience in the settings in which we place them. This belief is part of the rationale for the presentation of theoretical perspectives informing this project in chapter 2. In addition, within the field of early childhood, the particular developmental requirements and capacities of children under age three need more attention.[6] Likewise, other disciplines must acknowledge the importance of early childhood by extending their studies to include our youngest children. The hierarchy that has placed child care at the bottom of the public policy heap also exists in academic scholarship.

Implications for caregiving cannot be derived from child psychology or developmental theory alone. "In addition to theoretical assumptions about how children learn or develop . . . educational ideologies include value assumptions about what is . . . worthwhile" (Kohlberg & Mayer, 1972, p. 463). These values and assumptions must be more explicitly addressed in the literature concerning and directed toward child caregivers. Brian Vandenberg (1987b) observed that words like "love, care and compassion" don't occur in our professional texts:

> We use more professional and technical sounding terms like attachment, prosocial behavior and social skills management. But if we are afraid to use words like love and care in our journals and conferences, are we not participating in the tendency of a technologically driven society to depersonalize human life? (p.8)

A more interdisciplinary and multitheoretical approach might provide caregivers (and those who teach and study them) broader and more meaningful philosophical groundings for action—grounds which would legitimate a view of themselves as emotionally engaged. The practice of child care might then be philosophically and morally, as well as theoretically, driven. As Vandenberg (1987a) noted, "our sense of empathy and moral responsibility is grounded in the fact that others are with us in the world, also confronted with the mystery of Being. Empathy and morality are *existentially* given, not *epistemologically* acquired" (p. 7).

Broadening the theoretical and philosophical bases for group-based caregiving necessitates the inclusion of multiple, diverse voices. Responsive caregiving, as it has been described here, rests upon many of my own personal experiences and convictions. While I draw support from phenomenological, interactionist, feminist, and critical theories, the descriptions herein are reminiscent of child-rearing recommendations derived from studies of at-home, white, middle-class mothers. I must acknowledge that there can be wide cultural variations of the concept and practice of responsive caregiving.[7] These variations would be worthy of further study and discussion (including discussion among care-givers). I would like to see the presentation herein considered as the initiation of a conversation in which diverse conceptions of responsive caregiving might be explored, which would include documenting illustrative interactions which occur not just within families, but within group care settings.

The Caregivers

Day care has been studied largely as an environment for children; the role of day care as a work environment for adults re-mains virtually unstudied (Phillips, 1987b). National statistics that estimate a 42 percent annual turnover rate among child-care workers (Phillips, 1987b) point to the inadequacy of our attention to caregivers, the lack of recognition of their emotional labor, and a failure to address the constraints affecting their work. Sorely missing from the literature are investigations of caregivers' per-spectives on their own caring experiences, and the particular problematics they face in these "unnatural" contexts. This text is also lacking in this regard.

The ethical implications of the possibility that caregivers may feel betrayed by the account herein, as sympathetic as I have tried to make it, have been disturbing throughout this project. It has not been my goal to hurt caregivers, but to generate under-standings of the life-worlds wherein they assume responsibility for our most vulnerable children, who cannot speak on their own behalf. If caregivers are unfavorably portrayed here, it is because my first commitment has been to the children.

In addition, the emerging nature of the research project, "the moment-to-moment press" (Hatch, 1993) of doing interpre-tive research, and the constraints I perceived in my role as uni-versity instructor and researcher are partial explanations for the absence of caregivers' voices in this text, a limitation I ac-knowledge and am now in the process of addressing (see Leavitt, 1993a, 1993b).

My immersion into the lives of the infants and toddlers and their caregivers began significantly, not as a research project, but with the supervision of practicum students. Establishing cor-dial and supportive relations with local programs had been an on-going process since I moved to the community. The university was dependent on these programs for both research and practicum sites, as few infant-toddler programs exist. The caregivers welcomed my students, colleagues, and me as guests in their programs. I felt a strong need to "get along," not only for any present group of students, but on behalf of future students to be placed in these programs. It is quite possible that what I did (or didn't) in the interest of maintaining rapport was interpreted on the caregivers' part as acceptance of and agreement with their practices. Indeed, the act of placing students in their rooms in itself may have been reasonably interpreted as condoning caregivers' practices.

When I visited these programs, caregivers often engaged me in conversation, sometimes about themselves, their lives, their co-workers, their supervisors, and the children and their parents. Occasionally, they would seek my opinion regarding some child care practice. It was my interpretation that caregivers' questions were more an attempt at verification than information. For example, when I was asked about crying babies I would reply honestly, but sympathetically. I'd acknowledge how difficult it is when three or four babies are crying at once, and how sometimes it doesn't seem to matter what one does in response. But I believe in responding to babies' distress, picking them up as circumstances permitted. I'd add, in fact, research indicates that responding to babies' cries actually lessens their crying. Caregivers typically reasserted their position about not spoiling babies: "I'd have to be holding babies all day long." Due to the constraints of the situation, that is, students, parents, and other adults in the room, and the priority of attending to the children, the dictates of "good manners," and the desire to "get along" in order to preserve the situation, I refrained from pursuing the issue. Thus, the stories I now tell, for the most part, do not include the caregivers' perspectives.

These constraints acknowledged, it does not absolve me from my responsibility to the caregivers, who unsuspectingly welcomed me into their classrooms. It's not that I believe obtaining their stories would change my critique. Rather, their stories would illuminate those I've constructed.

Caregivers are participants in a system they did not create. What do they believe about their practices? They do not hide them from observers. Does this imply they believe in their legitimacy and appropriateness? How do caregivers define the conflicts they face and depict the choices they make in the course of their daily work? How do they speak about themselves, their co-workers, and the children?

Caregivers' perspectives are explored more fully in a study in progress, as I interview these and other caregivers. Issues I am exploring include caregivers' feelings about their work and the children, their philosophical beliefs about childhood and caregiving, their perceptions of problematic and rewarding experiences, and the ways in which their centers are satisfying and supportive (or not) working environments. I wonder how these caregivers found themselves in their jobs, how prepared they feel for their work, and how they negotiate the terrain of caregiving. How do caregivers try to maintain their own well-being while caring for the children? Over time, I have observed a few caregivers attempt to change their practices. I would like to understand what motivates, influences and guides these changes. I also wiil share some of the field notes included here and ask caregivers for their interpretations of them, at the same time sharing my own thoughts about them. In sum, the primary purpose of this project is to illuminate the meanings caregivers give to their work in their own words. These understandings are critical to any endeavor to care for caregivers.

The Children

Infants and toddlers have few means and little power to make their voices heard; a great deal of interpretive effort is involved in understanding their experiences. While I have attempted to view experience as much as possible from the child's perspective, I am aware that my adult interpretations of the children's experiences are limited by a tendency to process them through my own adult view of the world. Some days I was so emotionally affected by the children's experiences I had to leave a center (the children did not have this option). This illustrates one way in which I as observer was not separate from the observed.

The meaning and significance of the interactions described in this text may lie more with the children's interpretations of these events as they experience and make sense of them. In other words, the "effects" of caregivers' actions and inaction toward children may lie less in the set of actions per se than in the child's construction of those actions (see Kagan, Kearsley, & Zelazo, 1980, p. 165). I can only say that I have conscientiously striven to see the world through these children's eyes to understand the meanings of their experiences for them, and modestly hope to speak on their behalf. I have attempted to "bear witness," to give voice to the experiences of society's often silenced, ignored, or invisible members—our youngest children. It is my hope that I can move the reader as I have been moved, by the seriousness of the personal troubles and issues involved in infant-toddler day care.

CONCLUSION

This interpretation of problematic experiences related to power and emotion within infant-toddler day care centers is, of course, unfinished, to be taken up again (see Denzin, 1984, p. 9). In this exploration of the lived experiences of children, I have suggested that the personal troubles of these infants and toddlers be addressed as public issues (see Mills, 1959). In so doing, I hope that I have developed groundings for understanding and praxis, so that even our youngest children might feel "at home in the world" (Vandenberg, 1971, p. 63.)

APPENDIX
The Credibility of
Interpretive Studies

Some people speak of method greedily, demandingly; what
they want in work is method; to them it never seems rigorous
enough, formal enough. . . . The invariable fact is that a work
which constantly proclaims its will-to-method is ultimately
sterile. . . . [There is] no surer way to kill a great piece of research and send it to the great scrap heap of abandoned projects than Method.

Barthes, *The Rustle of Language*

It is with some reservation that I include this appendix,
as the preoccupation with validity concerns can have the effect of
transforming interpretive inquiry into a procedural variation of
quantitative inquiry, negating fundamental differences in both
assumptions and procedures (Smith, 1984; Smith & Heshusius,
1986). At the same time, I acknowledge the interest of some read-
ers in assessing the worthiness of interpretive research and
herein offer my own position.

The aims of interpretive studies are descriptive and particular, focused on revealing life experiences in concrete social situations (Denzin, 1982). As interpretive studies are emergent
inquiries, issues of validity, reliability, truth, falsity, objectivity,
generalizability, representativeness and replicability are understood differently than for quantitative or positivist studies (Denzin, 1982, 1989a, 1989b, 1989c; Genishi, 1982; Guba & Lincoln,
1982; Smith & Robbins, 1982). This does not, however, imply an
absence of criteria for evaluation of interpretive accounts. Judg-
ment about the quality of qualitative research rests upon the ad-
equacy of the data collection procedures, the detailed richness of
the descriptions, and the depth and quality of the interpretations
(Barritt, Beekman, Bleeker, & Mulderij, 1983; see also Polkinghorne, 1983).

The delineation of my immersion into the field of study indicates the extent to which I have met some of the criteria suggested by qualitative researchers. One of these is prolonged
engagement at the site(s) and persistent observation over time.
The field notes presented are grounded in the actual behaviors of

interacting individuals and represent repeated instances over time, sites, and observers.

The collection and interpretation of field notes has been an ongoing, interrelated process of pattern recognition or a search for emerging themes (Barritt, Beekman, Bleeker, & Mulderij, 1983; Genishi, 1982; Porter & Potenza, 1983; Smith & Robbins, 1982). "The'seeing' of the pattern which gives meaning to the text requires insight . . . " (Polkinghorne, 1983, p. 238). There are no hard and fast rules applied in the search for themes—criteria for what rates as a theme may relate to frequency of occurrence but also the perceived importance of events (Walsh, Baturka, Smith, & Cotter, 1989).

The singularity or infrequency of an occurrence is not a justification for assigning it insignificance. Some parts of experience are simply unique, but no less important or valuable in terms of generating insight into and understanding of the phenomena. Gadamer (1975) speaks to this issue: in

> modern science . . . experience is valid only if it is confirmed; hence its dignity depends on its fundamental repeatability. But this means that experience by its very nature abolishes its history. (p. 311)

Each case in an interpretive study can be regarded as a "universal singular" (Sartre, 1971/1981), a dramatic instance of what may occur elsewhere in similar settings, typical in a more real sense than can be verified by a statistical calculation. "It is typical . . . in the same way that every case is representative of its kind . . . the study of the experiences of one person at the same time reveals the life-activities of his/her group" (Burgess, 1966, pp. 185–86; cited in Denzin, 1989c, p. 171).

The believability, or verisimilitude, of the thick descriptions is another criteria for the soundness of the study. Verisimilitude is achieved when the reader is able to feel and sense the flow of interaction, that is, when the experiences of those being studied come alive in the mind of the reader (Denzin, 1982; 1989a). The field notes presented herein are "reliable" in the sense that these observations, as public behaviors, could have been made by any similarly situated observer (Denzin, 1989c). I take the position of Suransky (1977):

> I have no desire to prove the replicability of my findings—they speak to me with sufficient power as they stand now. . . . I would earnestly encourage those who are so inclined to take upon

themselves the task of further investigating the lives of children in such settings. . . . I believe that what I have seen is symbolic of the larger child care milieu—but that belief remains to be challenged or supported by future endeavors. (pp. 8–9)

That I have made a serious attempt to uncover my underlying theoretical assumptions, biases, and prior understandings is another measure of the credibility of this report. Finally, the project is also judged by its contributions to understanding, the extent to which I have opened "horizons of meaning" and made intelligible children's lived experience and provoked thought related to that experience.

Notes

CHAPTER 1

1. See D. E. Smith (1979, 1987) for an elaboration of her understanding of the everyday world as a sociological problematic, as well as Waksler (1986) regarding her suggestions to study childhood socialization as problematic.

2. See also Schutz's (1967) discussion on the taken-for-granted: "that particular level of experience which presents itself as not in need of further analysis" (p. 74).

3. In Sartre's view, "emotion is simply a way by which consciousness chooses to live its relationship to the world" (Barnes, 1956, p. xvii).

4. The period of infancy, although sometimes used to indicate all children under three years of age, here refers to children generally under twelve to fifteen months, or those not yet walking. Children are generally considered toddlers as they become mobile; state licensing standards for day care centers define them between fifteen and twenty-four months old, although in the literature two-year-olds are included.

5. I generally use the term *day care* to refer specifically to institutions or group-care programs that take in children on a daily, temporary basis. Although the hours of program service may extend from eight to ten hours or longer, children return home each evening. *Child care* refers to that act or set of behaviors that is to occur within day care centers, as well as other settings.

6. It is difficult to obtain an exact count of how many children under age three are actually enrolled in day care centers, as most statistics seem to focus on the number of their working mothers and the arrangements they make, rather than the number of children recorded by age as enrolled in programs. What is clear, however, is that the number of our youngest children enrolled in center-based day care programs is increasing.

7. See Harkness and Super (1983) for a discussion of the interest in children in terms of their future functioning as adults, over a concern for the ongoing life of the child.

8. My initial, working knowledge of day care stemmed from my own experiences as a caregiver and center director. Graduate studies and university work have complemented and modified those understandings developed in personal experience. It is these prejudices that I have brought with me into the sites of study, although I have tried to bracket them as much as possible in developing sympathetic understandings of other persons' lived situations. I admit to a distinct political commitment and a particular involvement in the subject; I have not attempted to stand outside the experiences I am trying to understand. This is not an attempt to transform personal opinion into authorized knowledge, but an attempt to develop grounded understandings while acknowledging there is no value-free inquiry.

9. Centers 1 and 2 were privately owned, enrolling about 55–75 children each. In center 1, the clientele tended toward the "professional," two-working-parents family. Center 2 served a broader range, including low-income and single parents; this center has recently gone out of business. Centers 3 and 4 are nonprofit and housed in churches; they serve a variety of families and are partially subsidized by federal funds. Center 3 is one of the largest local centers, enrolling as many as 176 children, a considerable proportion from low-income, culturally diverse, and single-parent families. Center 4 has a capacity for 71 children and serves a considerable number of academic and professional families, although it is the only one of the six with a sliding fee scale. Center 5 is the newest, a corporate-sponsored program with a capacity for 142 children. Center 6 is a for-profit program affiliated with a national chain, with a capacity for 123 children.

10. Some question how "natural" individuals are when observed, concerned about the "reactive effects" of participant observation (Denzin, 1989c). I acknowledge this varies by degrees but contend that my extended contact over time in these programs, and the maintenance of positive relations, contributed to the eventual relaxing of caregivers in my presence. Indeed, they did not hesitate to ignore or yell at children while I visited; they often discussed their personal lives with me and complained about other caregivers and center administration. This "relaxing" was similar to what occurred during another participant-observation study I conducted of family day care homes in which some caregivers were partially dressed or fell asleep in the researchers' presence (Eheart & Leavitt, 1989). I firmly believe my presence became taken for granted in both these studies. At any rate, the interpretive stance posits the impossibility of separating the observer from the observed. The reactive ef-

fect can be evaluated to some extent by the field notes (Denzin, 1989c); the data stands on its own for the reader to assess.

11. For a more in-depth review of studies addressing infant day care, see Belsky (1984, 1985); Belsky and Steinberg (1978); Belsky, Steinberg and Walker (1982); Caldwell and Freyer (1982); Clarke-Stewart (1982); Clarke-Stewart and Fein (1983); Fein and Fox (1988); Gamble and Zigler (1986); Kagan, Kearsley, and Zelazo, (1980); Kilmer (1979); see also the collection of articles in Ainslie (1984).

12. See references cited in text, particularly Rutter (1981) as well as Bretherton and Waters (1985), for more information.

13. Day care after a child's first year is not part of this debate, as there has been very little research specifically addressing toddlerhood (Eheart, in press). For the few exceptions, see Howes (1987), Rubenstein and Howes (1983), and Whitebook, Howes, and Phillips (1989). These studies generally conclude that the quality of care is variable, but that emotional development is generally unimpaired as a function of day care.

14. Overlooked in this debate over the ecological validity and inter-pretation of the Strange Situation as a procedure to assess the effects of infant day care are the *ethics* of this laboratory procedure. This proce-dure's sequence of separations and reunions is *purposely* designed to be *stressful* for the infants, in an attempt to measure the extent to which he or she seeks comfort from the mother. I contend that this exercise of power over the infant in the name of science is unethical, as it manipu-lates and objectifies its subjects. While infants generally have little say about the experiences to which they are subjected, most often adults can rationalize their actions by appealing to developmental goals or situa-tional practicalities. In this case, justification is questionable, especially since there are alternative approaches to assess children's experiences in day care.

15. See Ehrenreich and English (1978), Lewin (1984), Shields and Koster (1989), and Willard (1988).

16. Yet there are studies of paternal *un*employment (see Bronfen-brenner & Crouter, 1982).

17. See Rhodes (1979) for a discussion not only of how day care re-search, but child development research and theory, reflects a cultural bias in favor of mother-at-home raised children.

18. See Power (1985a) for further discussion regarding the inade-quacy of decontextualized, quantitative studies of children's emotional-ity. For a broader perspective on theoretical approaches to the study of emotions, see Cirillo, Kaplan, and Wapner (1989); Denzin (1984, 1985); Fogel (1980); Franks and McCarthy (1989); Gordon (1981, 1985); Lewis and Saarni (1985); Parke (1979); Power (1985b, 1986); Saarni and Harris (1989); Shott (1979); and Yarrow (1979); among others.

19. I do not wish to deny, oversimplify, or overlook the contributions of these studies. I wish to point out, however, that there are limitations to them (as well as to my own), and to suggest that there are other ways to assess children's experiences and development.

20. For examples, see Anderson, Nagle, Roberts, and Smith (1981); Belsky (1985); Clarke-Stewart (1984, 1987, 1988); Clarke-Stewart and Gruber (1984); Fox and Fein (1988); Frye (1982); and Zimiles (1986).

21. See Bronfenbrenner (1979), Caldwell and Freyer (1982), Clarke-Stewart and Fein (1983), Porter and Potenza (1983), and Scarr (1979).

CHAPTER 2

1. I acknowledge that there are other directions from which to approach the project I have undertaken, and other texts to be applied in the interpretation of children's experiences. (For example, I could have interpreted the experiences described herein solely in terms of Dewey's philosophical works on experience, education, and freedom.) My choices have emerged as part of my personal biography and my professional and graduate school journey into theoretical arenas, which has been eclectic and is by no means complete nor comprehensive. The interpretive process is a circle in which I have intersected with many texts simultaneously, and in which my understandings are admittedly incomplete. See Bernstein (1978), Denzin (1989a), Manen (1990), and Mills (1959) regarding personal saliency as a starting point of research.

2. I have relied on several texts in compiling this section. Primary texts applied in this section are Barrit, Beekman, Bleeker, and Mulderij (1983), Denzin (1982, 1989a, 1989b), Hoy (1988), Manen (1990), Packer (1985, 1987), and Warren (1984). See also Gadamer (1975, 1976). See Bleicher (1980) for an overview of the main strands of contemporary hermeneutic thought; Schroeder (1984) for a critical examination of the theories of Sartre, Heidegger, Husserl, and Hegel; and Tesch (1985) for an extensive bibliography on phenomenology, existentialism, hermeneutics, and ethnography; as well as the bibliographies found in sources cited.

3. In the interests of reducing wordiness, from here on I will use the terms "interpretive studies" or "interpretive perspectives" to refer to the family of hermeneutic, existential phenomenology, and later to include in this family the interactionist, critical, feminist, and postmodern perspectives. Precedence for such an encompassing move has been made by Denzin (1989a). Such a move is not intended to discount the variations among and between these families of thought.

4. Geertz (1973) is most well known for the term "thick description." I, however, primarily follow Denzin's (1989a) understanding of this term.

5. Denzin (1989a) has demonstrated the compatibility of joining symbolic interactionist thought with the traditions of hermeneutics and phenomenology.

6. See also Mead (1934/1962), Cooley (1909/1937, 1922), Dewey (1929/1958, 1929/1960, 1931/1963) and James (1907/1981). Exposition of the philosophy of pragmatism is beyond the scope of this presentation, its relationship to symbolic interactionism notwithstanding.

7. See Berger and Luckmann (1967) on the "reflected self," Cooley (1922) on the "looking glass self," and Mead (1934/1962) on taking the attitude of the other.

8. This paragraph derives primarily from Denzin's (1977) text, *Childhood Socialization*.

9. For more in-depth discussion and history of critical theory see Bernstein (1978), Bredo and Feinberg (1982), Habermas (1968/1971), and Jay (1973), among others, as well as the sources cited in text.

10. At the same time commonalities are noted, feminists point out the masculine bias within these perspectives and the neglect of gender issues (e.g., Fraser, 1989). Others argue (more problematically, perhaps) that the historical concerns and priorities of women derive from women's unique experiences and provide a source for a distinctly female critique of human institutions and social relationships (see Grimshaw, 1986).

11. R. Steele (1989) contends that the "hermeneutic gaze—a critically interpretive approach" (p. 224)—is akin to feminist consciousness-raising: a transformation of seeing, understanding, and feeling.

12. Feminist philosophy, like those previously discussed, is not a unified or homogenous discourse but it is possible to identify some common themes (Flax, 1987). Primary sources relied on for this section include Cook and Fonow (1986); De Lauretis (1986); Farganis (1986); Grimshwaw (1986); Harding (1987); Keohane, Rosaldo, and Gelpi (1981); Martin (1988); Pateman and Gross (1986); Stanley and Wise (1983); and Treichler (1986); in addition to those sources cited in the text.

13. A difference between the "undistorting" of critical research and the "consciousness-raising" of feminism can be seen in the degree of *reciprocal* enlightenment, or equal status and expertise attributed to the researcher and "subject." Critical theory can be criticized for its tone of vanguardism, as well as one of condescension and superiority.

14. At the same time I draw from feminist theory I am cautious about appealing to a feminist ethic or morality of care insofar as such appeals are couched in terms of women's "instinct," "nature," or "distinctive experience."

15. Central figures of postmodern thought include, but are certainly not limited to, Barthes (1957/1972, 1986), Baudrillard (1983a, 1983b), Foucault (1975/1979a, 1980), and Lyotard (1979/1984). Postmodern

thought encompasses poststructuralism (Young, 1981), cultural studies (Hall, 1980), semiotics (Baudrillard, 1981; Denzin, 1986b, 1987a), and deconstruction (Derrida, 1967/1978, 1976, 1981). Details of these divergences are beyond the scope of this project.

16. There is some debate as to whether postmodernism is simply another movement *within* rather than a *break* from modernism, as "the project of modernity has never been without its critics" (Harvey, 1989, p. 15; see also Balbus, 1988; Berman, 1988; Foster, 1983; and Hoy, 1988). The meaning of modernism is also confused; it has not been a static body of thought—it encompasses many changes and challenges. This point acknowledged, I continue to discuss postmodernism as a distinctive movement in response to modernism, as there has certainly been a distinct body of literature taking up these themes under the name of postmodernism (see Huyssen, 1984).

17. Critics of postmodernism note its own tendencies to be totalizing and hegemonic (McLaren, 1991), in spite of these admonitions.

18. I freely admit to modernist concerns (see Berman, 1988), and draw from traditional "grand" theories, as problematic as they have been shown to be. Hoy (1988) wrote that "the same person, discipline, or institution can be traditional in some respects, modern in others, and postmodern in yet others" (p. 38). Stuhr (1990) suggests "we explore postmodern accounts of subjects and cultural formations given traditional pragmatic commitments to humanism, liberalism and community" (p. 657).

19. Rabinow & Sullivan (1979) portray earlier critical theory as taking a more pessimistic, postmodern tone: a "negative dialectic" with little chance to recover a more fully human existence.

20. The worthiness of a pluralistic theoretical and methodological approach has been noted by Howard (1983) and Roth (1987), among others.

CHAPTER 3

1. Foucault's concept of disciplinary time parallels Weber's definition of discipline: "the practiced nature of uncritical and unresisting *mass* obedience" (Weber, 1962, p. 117).

2. By no means do I intend to imply that the "culture of silence" for children in day care centers in the United States is comparable to the extreme physical, political, and economic oppression and violence experienced in Central and South America and other "Third World" societies to which Freire typically refers. Examining the ways in which children are enculturated from early infancy, however, illuminates how the imposition of oppressive ideologies, whatever the degree, are ingrained in our

everyday, taken-for-granted practices, including those situated in day care centers.

3. Sommerville (1990) notes that with the suggestion that it is *nature* which subdues and manipulates the child Emile, his tutor "feels free to dominate the child more completely than if he had to acknowledge his use of power" (p. 154).

4. See Hill (1987), K. B. Jones (1988), and Meyers (1987) for discussions related to the complimentary rather than oppositional relationship between authority and autonomy.

5. Johnson (1990) points out that one of the main criteria by which teachers are judged is their ability to keep "order" in the classroom. See also Silberman (1970) on the "school's preoccupation with order and control" (pp. 113–57).

CHAPTER 4

1. I realize some will object to the attribution of emotions to young infants, as there is some debate as to when infants feel and become aware of "true" emotions (see Yarrow, 1979). Infants are, however, immediately drawn into the emotional culture and are sensitive and responsive to the feelings of their caregivers.

2. See Leavitt and Power (1989) for another description of children regarded as objects, or nonpersons, by caregivers during emotional interactions. This lack of emotional identification and reciprocity is discussed in the context of postmodernism.

3. See Liljestrom (1983) on the degradation of emotional life, as emotions are considered irrational, private, and "childish" in the negative sense. It appears that even children may not be allowed this childishness.

4. Noddings (1984) acknowledges that even within "natural circles" (p. 52) caregivers often experience conflicts and may feel burdened.

5. Hochschild (1983) distinguishes between emotional *labor* and emotion *work*, the management of feelings in a *private* context. See also Goffman (1967) on the affectation of involvement.

6. The Marxist sense of alienation may be insufficient, however, in understanding the caregivers' behavior. It "presupposes a coherent rather than a fragmented sense of self from which to be alienated" (Harvey, 1989, p. 53). From a postmodern standpoint, our way of being in the world is fragmented and unstable; "alienation of the subject is displaced by fragmentation of the subject" (Jameson, 1984, p. 63, cited in Harvey, 1989, p. 54). In this view, the caregiver approaches her work *already* fragmented, as a product of our postmodern society.

7. The effects of this isolation, even for eight hours, should not be underrated. When I worked on a daily basis with infants and toddlers I found that my vocabulary and the range of topics in which I might converse with adults diminished considerably. I often found myself talking to adults in the same tone I used with toddlers. My own world in which I could feel myself to be an interesting, effective adult was shrinking. This was compounded by my sensitivity to the public perception that my work was of low status, unskilled "babysitting," despite my advanced education.

8. See Schwalbe (1986) regarding how capitalist labor processes preclude regard for the well-being of others.

9. It has been questioned whether children, as not "fully constituted" beings, can be alienated. I posit that this "constitution" is a lifelong process beginning with the birth of the feeling, experiencing, constructing, and constructed being. "The child as a conscious *becoming* being pursues a 'project' of freedom in order to become some-one himself and not a being for others" (Vandenberg, 1971, cited in Suransky, 1977, p. 262). Insofar as a child is thwarted in the process of constructing an authentic self, he or she experiences alienation.

10. Loseke is referring to family day-care providers, as they intend to be "second mothers" to the children in care (see also Eheart & Leavitt, 1989). Nevertheless, the comments apply to center-based caregivers.

11. See Lief and Fox (1963) regarding the idea of "detached concern" in the caring professions, and Katz (1980) regarding the "optimum detachment" called for in early childhood programs.

12. This argument does not necessarily depend on a notion of an already existing "essential self." The child's self is one that, in always becoming, always is. "The self is not in consciousness, but rather in experience and in the interpersonal relationships that bind the person to others" (Sullivan, 1953, cited in Denzin, 1989b, p. 31).

13. See Berger and Luckmann (1967) on the "reflected self," Cooley (1922) on the "looking-glass self," and Mead (1934/1962) on taking the attitude of the other.

CHAPTER 5

1. These are philosophical assertions, theoretical and empirical evidence notwithstanding. My intent is not to argue the "truth" of this proposition but to explore what it might mean in the context of day care.

2. See Schutz (1967) on intersubjective understanding: putting oneself in the place of the other and identifying our lived experience with the other's. Shott (1979) also defines empathy as imagining how another feels or what another's situation is like.

3. Adapted from Gonzalez-Mena and Eyer (1993, pp. 52).

4. This scene is revised from a description of child-centered guidance in Reynolds (1990, p. 99).

5. See Mead (1934/1962) regarding how "taking the attitude of the other" makes possible the emergence of the "self."

6. This is not to say that our understandings are complete nor unproblematic. Interdisciplinary and multitheoretical perspectives on child development and socialization have yielded considerable insights, however, which have provided tentative bases for action. The postmodern assertion that "there is no absolute to guide action which is not . . . provisional" (Ryan, 1982, p. 81) does not have to be paralyzing, but can serve instead to inspire further study, reflection, and conversation, as we act on continually emerging understandings.

7. Mixed-age groups occur already in most family day care homes (which is not to say some of the same problems described here don't also occur in these homes; see Eheart & Leavitt, 1989) Long-term mixed-age grouping is not a *sufficient* condition, but may be a *facilitative* one, for responsive caregiving. The Bank Street Family Center in New York groups infants and toddlers together with no transition until age three (see Balaban, 1991). Children also stay in the same group for three years in Italy (New, 1990).

8. I acknowledge there are some male caregivers. But these are by far in the minority, especially in infant care. Ninety-seven percent of the caregivers surveyed in the National Child Care Staffing Study (Whitebook, Howes, & Phillips, 1989) were female.

9. See Freire's (1970) discussion of "conscientization" (p. 19). See Reynolds' (1990) discussion of the problem-solving staff meeting in child care programs (pp. 263–77). She suggests role-playing as one way to develop caregivers' capacities for perspective-taking. See Schon (1983) on the process of problem solving and becoming a "reflective practitioner."

10. See Gilligan and Wiggins (1988) regarding the differences between a justice framework where care is a matter of obligations and duties, and a care framework, in which justice becomes a matter of self-care as well as other care. See also Gilligan's (1988) conception of a feminist morality of care. In my appeal to a feminist ethic of care I am not taking on the debate as to whether the two moral orientations (justice and care) are in fact distinct and gender-based.

CHAPTER 6

1. Indeed, interactions similar to those described here may very well take place within children's family homes. My intention has not been to

compare home-reared with day-care children. Likewise, I don't mean to portray what is described here as *all* that happens in child care programs. Surely there are other, and sometimes, happier, stories to be told. These stories also need to be documented, for the insights they might provide regarding responsive caregiving.

2. See Bowles and Gintis (1976) and Giroux (1987), among others, for more discussion of the relationship between technocratic, rationalist ideology and schooling.

3. See Badinter (1980), Birns and Hay (1988), and Dally (1982).

4. See Clarke-Stewart's (1982) historical overview, as well as Steinfels (1973) and Suransky (1977, 1982), among others. See Martinez (1989) for a history of the inconsistent, fragmented federal role in childcare policy.

5. These phrases reflect a view of children as commodities and are indicative of our little regard for children as beings-for-themselves and for their present lived experience. See Grubb & Lazerson (1982, pp. 53–58) for a discussion of this instrumental view of children.

6. Howes (1987) notes that while child development and early childhood education programs have focused on preschool-age children for years, we lag behind in attention to infant-toddler care.

7. See, for example, Polakow (1992) study of preschool-age day care, specifically the chapter including field notes from a predominantly black, low-income day care program. Polakow describes several adult-child interactions which, on the surface, would appear poor examples of responsive caregiving in a "professional" child-care program. But their significance lies in their authenticity, the lack of professional, distancing jargon and technique. The caregivers were authentically, emotionally engaged with the children and (key) the children seemed to understand the adults' words and actions as protective and loving.

References

Ainslie, R. (Ed.). (1984). *The child and the day care setting*: *Qualitative variations and development*. New York: Praeger.

Ainsworth, M. D. S. (1964). Patterns of attachment behavior shown by the infant in interaction with his mother. *Merrill-Palmer Quarterly* 10: 51–58.

————(1970). Attachment, exploration, and separation illustrated by the behavior of one-year-olds in a strange situation. *Child Development* 41: 49–67.

————(1973). The development of infant-mother attachment. In B. Caldwell & M. Ricciuti (Eds.), *Review of child development research, vol. 3: Child development and social policy* (pp. 1–94). Chicago: University of Chicago Press.

————(1979). Infant-mother attachment. *American Psychologist* 34: 932–37.

Ainsworth, M. D.; Blehar, M.; Waters, E.; & Wall, S. (1978). *Patterns of attachment*: *Observations in the strange situation and at home*. Hillsdale, N.J.: Lawrence Erlbaum.

Anderson, C. W.; Nagle, R. J.; Roberts, W. A.; & Smith, J. W. (1981). Attachment to substitute caregivers as a function of center quality and caregiver involvement. *Child Development* 52: 53–61.

Badinter, E. (1980). *Mother love*: *Myth and reality*. New York: Macmillan.

Balaban, N. (1991). Mainstreamed, mixed-age groups of infants and toddlers and the Bank Street Family Center. *Zero to Three* 11 (3): 13–16.

Balbus, I. D. (1988). Disciplining women: Michael Foucault and the power of feminist discourse. In J. Arac (Ed.), *After Foucault: Humanistic knowledge, postmodern challenges* (pp. 138–60). New Brunswick: Rutgers University Press.

Barnes, H. (1956). Translator's introduction. In J. P. Sartre, *Being and nothingness* (pp. ix–lii). New York: Simon & Schuster.

Barritt, L.; Beekman, T.; Bleeker, H.; & Mulderij, K. (1983). *A handbook for phenomenological research in education*. Ann Arbor: University of Michigan School of Education.

Barthes, R. (1972). *Mythologies* (A. Lavers, Trans.). New York: Hill & Wang. (Original work published 1957.)

———(1979). From work to text. In J. V. Harari (Ed.), *Textual Strategies* (pp. 73-81). Ithica, NY: Cornell University Press.

———(1986). *The rustle of language* (R. Howard, Trans.). New York: Hill & Wang.

Baudrillard, J. (1981). *For a critique of the political economy of the sign*. St. Louis: Telos Press.

———(1983a). *Simulations* (P. Foss, P. Patton, & P. Beitchman, Trans.). New York: Semiotext(e).

———(1983b). Ecstacy of communication. In H. Foster (Ed.), *The anti-aesthetic: Essays on postmodern culture* (pp. 126–34). Port Townsend, Wash.: Bay Press.

Becker, H. (1973). *Outsiders*. New York: The Free Press.

Beekman, T. (1983). Human science as dialogue with children. *Phenomonology and Pedagogy* 1.

Belsky, J. (1984). Two waves of day care research: Developmental effects and conditions of quality. In R. Ainslie (Ed.), *The child and the day care setting: Qualitative variations and development* (pp. 1–34). New York: Praeger.

———(1985). The science and politics of day care. In R. L. Shotland & M. M. Mark (Eds.), *Social science and social policy* (pp. 237–62). Beverly Hills, Calif.: Sage.

———(1986). Infant day care: A cause for concern? *Zero to Three* 7 (1): 1–7.

———(1988). The effects of infant day care reconsidered. *Early Childhood Research Quarterly* 3: 235–72.

———(1989). Infant-parent attachment and day care: In defense of the strange situation. In J. S. Lande, S. Scarr, & N. Gunzenhauser (Eds.), *Caring for children: Challenge to America* (pp. 23–47). Hillsdale, N.J.: Lawrence Erlbaum.

Belsky, J., & Steinberg, L. (1978). The effects of day care: A critical review. *Child Development* 49: 929–49.

Belsky, J.; Steinberg, L.; & Walker, A. (1982). The ecology of day care. In M. Lamb (Ed.), *Nontraditional families: Parenting and child development* (pp. 71–116). New Jersey: Lawrence Erlbaum.

Benn, R. (1986). Factors promoting secure attachment relationships between employed mothers and their sons. *Child Development* 57: 1224–31.

Benson, C. (no date). *Who cares for kids? A report on child care providers*. Washington, D.C.: National Commission on Working Women.

Berger, P., & Luckmann, T. (1967). *The social construction of reality*. New York: Anchor.

Bergmann, F. (1977). *On being free*. Notre Dame, Ind.: University of Indiana Press.

Berman, M. (1988). Why modernism still matters. *Tikkun* 4 (1): 11–14, 81–86.

Bernstein, R. J. (1978). *The restructuring of social and political theory*. Philadelphia: University of Pennsylvania Press.

Birns, B., & Hay, D. F. (1988). Introduction. In B. Birns & D. Hay (Eds.), *The different faces of motherhood* (pp. 1–9). New York: Plenum Press.

Bleicher, J. (1980). *Contemporary hermeneutics*. London: Routledge & Kegan Paul.

Block, M., & Block, J. (1980). Women and the dialectics of nature in eighteenth century French thought. In C. P. McCormack & M. Strathern (Eds.), *Nature, culture and gender* (pp. 25–41). Cambridge: Cambridge University Press.

Blumer, H. (1969). *Symbolic interactionism: Perspective and method*. Berkeley: University of California Press.

Bowlby, J. (1958). The nature of the child's tie to his mother. *International Journal of Psychoanalysis* 39: 350–73

———(1969). *Attachment and loss, vol. 1: Attachment*. New York: Basic.

———(1973). *Attachment and loss, vol. 2: Separation*. New York: Basic.

Bowles, S., & Gintis, H. (1976). *Schooling in capitalist America: Educational reform and the contradiction of economic life*. New York: Basic.

Bowman, B. (1989). Self-reflection as an element of professionalism. *Teachers College Record* 90 (3): 444–51.

Bredo, E., & Feinberg, W. (Eds.). (1982). *Knowledge and values in social and educational research*. Philadelphia: Temple University.

Bretherton, I., & Waters, E. (Eds.). (1985). Growing points of attachment theory and research. *Monographs of the Society for Research in Child Development* 50 (1–2, serial no. 209).

Bronfenbrenner, U. (1979). Contexts of childrearing: Problems and prospects. *American Psychologist* 34 (10): 844–50.

Bronfenbrenner, U., & Crouter, A. (1982). Work and family through time and space. In S. Kammerman & E. Hayes (Eds.), *Families that work: Children in a changing world* (pp. 39–83). Washington, D.C.: National Academy Press.

Burgess, E. (1966). Discussion. In C. Shaw, *The jack-roller*. Chicago: University of Chicago Press.

Cahill, S. (1990, April). *Emotionality, morality, selves, and societies*. Comments prepared for the "Sociology of Emotions in Post-Modern America" session of the 1990 annual meetings of the Midwest Sociologial Society, Chicago, Ill.

Cahill, S., & Loseke, D. (1990). *Disciplining the littlest ones: Popular day care discourse in post-war America*. Paper presented at the annual meetings of the Society for Symbolic Interactionism, Washington, D.C.

Calder, P. (1985). Children in nurseries. In C. New & M. David (Eds.), *For the children's sake: Making child care more than women's business* (pp. 243–70). New York: Penguin Books.

Caldwell, B., & Freyer, M. (1982). Day care and early education. In B. Spodek (Ed.), *Handbook of research in early childhood education* (pp. 21–43). New York: Free Press.

Cann, C. H. (1987). Women, organizations and power. In J. Sharistanian (Ed.), *Beyond the public/domestic dichotomy: Contemporary perspectives on women's public lives* (pp. 11–31). New York:Greenwood Press.

Caputo, J. (1987). *Radical hermeneutics: Repetition, deconstruction, and the hermeneutic project*. Bloomington: University of Indiana Press.

Castañeda, H. N. (1989). Philosophy as a science and as a world view. In A. Cohen & M. Dascal (Eds.), *The institution of philosophy: A discipline in crisis?* Lasalle, Ill.: Open Court.

Chase-Lansdale, P. L., & Owen, M. T. (1987). Maternal employment in a family context: Effects on infant-mother and infant-father attachments. *Child Development* 58: 1505–12.

Chess, S. (1987). Comments: Infant day care: A cause for concern? *Zero to Three* 7 (3): 24–25.

Child Care Action Campaign. (1988). Child care: The bottom line. *Child Care ActioNews* 5 (5): 1.

Cirillo, V.; Kaplan, B.; & Wapner, S. (Eds.) (1989). *Emotions in ideal human development*. Hillsdale, N.J.: Lawrence Erlbaum.

Clarke-Stewart, A. (1977). *Child care in the family: A review of research and some propositions for policy*. New York: Academic Press.

———(1982). *Day care*. Cambridge, Mass.: Harvard University Press.

———(1984). Day care: A new context for research and development. In M. Perlmutter (Ed.), *Parent-child interaction and parent-child relations in child development* (pp. 61–100). Hillsdale, N.J.:Lawrence Erlbaum.

————(1987). In search of consistencies in child care research. In D. Phillips (Ed.), *Quality in child care: What does the research tell us?* (pp. 105–19). Washington, D.C.: National Association for the Education of Young Children.

————(1988). The "effects" of infant day care reconsidered *Early Childhood Research Quarterly* 3 (3): 293–318.

Clarke-Stewart, A., & Fein, G. (1983). Early childhood programs. In M. Haith & J. Campos (Eds.), *Handbook of child psychology, vol. 2: Infancy and developmental psychology* (pp. 917–99). New York: Wiley.

Clarke-Stewart, A., & Gruber, C. (1984). Day care forms and features. In R. Ainslie (Ed.), *The child and the day care setting* (pp. 35–62). New York: Praeger.

Clifford, J. (1986). Introduction: Partial truths. In J. Clifford & G. Marcus (Eds.), *Writing culture: The poetics and politics of ethnography* (pp. 1–26). Berkeley: University of California Press.

Colapietro, V. (1990). The vanishing subject of contemporary discourse: A pragmatic response. *The Journal of Philosophy* 90: 644–55.

Coles, R. (1967). *Children of crisis, vol. 2: Migrants, sharecroppers, mountaineers.* Boston: Little, Brown.

Comstock, D. (1982). A method for critical research. In E. Bredo & W. Feinberg (Eds.), *Knowledge and values in social and educational research* (pp. 370–90). Philadelphia: Temple University.

Cook, J., & Fonow, M. (1986). Knowledge and women's interests: Issues of epistemology and methodology in feminist sociological research. *Sociological Inquiry* 56 (1): 2–29.

Cooley, C. H. (1922). *Human nature and the social order.* NewYork: Scribner.

————(1937). *Social organization.* New York: Scribner. (Original work published 1909.)

Dally, A. (1982). *Inventing motherhood: The consequences of an ideal.* London: Burnett Books.

De Lauretis, T. (Ed.). (1986). *Feminist studies/critical studies.* Bloomington, Ind: Indiana University Press.

Denzin, N. K. (1973a). The politics of childhood. In N. K.Denzin (Ed.), *Children and their caretakers* (pp. 1–25). New Brunswick, N.J.: E. P. Dutton.

————(1973b). The work of little children. In N. K. Denzin (Ed.), *Children and their caretakers* (pp. 117–26). New Brunswick, N.J.: E. P. Dutton.

————(1977). *Childhood socialization.* San Francisco: Jossey-Bass.

————(1982). Contributions of anthropology and sociology to qualitative research methods. In E. Kuhns & S.V. Martorana (Eds.), *New direc-*

tions for institutional research: *Qualitative methods for institutional research, no. 34* (pp. 17–26). San Francisco: Jossey Bass.

———(1984). *On understanding emotion*. San Francisco: Jossey-Bass.

———(1985). Emotion as lived experience. *Symbolic Interaction* 8 (2): 223–40.

———(1986a). Postmodern social theory. *Sociological Theory* 4: 194–204.

———(1986b). On a semiotic approach to mass culture. *American Journal of Sociology* 92: 678–83.

———(1987a). On semiotics and symbolic interactionism. *Symbolic Interactionism* 10 (1): 1–19.

———(1987b, March/April). Postmodern children. *Society: 32–35.*

———(1989a). *Interpretive interactionism*. Newbury Park, Calif.: Sage.

———(1989b). *Interpretive biography*. Newbury Park, Calif.: Sage.

———(1989c). *The research act: A theoretical introduction to sociological methods*. Englewood Cliffs, N.J.: Prentice Hall.

———(1990). Harold and Agnes: A feminist narrative undoing. *Sociological Theory* 8: 198–216.

Derrida, J. (1976). *Of grammatology* (G. C. Spivak, Trans.). Baltimore: Johns Hopkins.

———(1978). *Writing and difference* (A. Bass, Trans.). Chicago: Routledge & Kegan Paul. (Original work published 1967.)

(1981). *Positions*. Chicago: University of Chicago Press.

Dewey, J. (1938). *Experience and education*. New York: Macmillan.

———(1956). *The school and society*. Chicago: University of Chicago Press. (Original work published 1900.)

———(1958). *Experience and nature*. New York: Dover. (Original work published 1929.)

———(1960). *Quest for certainty: A study in the relation of knowledge and action*. New York: Capricorn Books. (Original work published 1929.)

———(1963). *Philosophy and civilization*. New York: Capricorn Books. (Original work published 1931.)

Diamond, I., & Quinby, L. (1988). *Feminism and Foucault: Reflections on resistance*. Boston: Northeastern University Press.

Diller, A. (1988). The ethics of care and education: A new paradigm, its critics, and its educational significance. *Curriculum Inquiry* 18 (3): 325–41.

Eheart, B. K. (in press). Toddler programs. In T. Husen & T. N. Postlewaite (Eds.), *International encyclopedia of education research and studies* (2d edition). Oxford, England: Pergamon.

Eheart, B. K., & Leavitt, R. L. (1989). Family day care: Discrepancies between intended and observed caregiving practices. *Early Childhood Research Quarterly* 4, (1) 145–62.

Ehrenreich, B., & English, D. (1978). *For her own good: 150 years of the experts' advice to women.* Garden City: Anchor Press/Doubleday.

Elshtain, J. B. (1981). *Public man, private woman: Women in social and political thought.* New Jersey: Princeton University.

Farganis, S. (1986). Social theory and feminist theory: The need for dialogue. *Sociological Inquiry* 56: 50–68.

Featherstone, M. (1988). In pursuit of the postmodern: An introduction. *Theory, Culture and Society* 5: 195–215.

Fein, G., & Fox, N. (Eds.). (1988). Infant day care. *Special Issue: Early Childhood Research Quarterly* 3 (3) and (4).

Flax, J. (1987). Postmodernism and gender relations in feminist theory. *Signs: Journal of Women in Culture and Society* 12 (4): 621–43.

Fogel, A. (1980). The role of emotion in early childhood education. In L. Katz (Ed.), *Current topics in early childhood education, vol. 3* (pp. 1–14). Norwood, N.J.: Ablex.

Foster, H. (1983). Postmodernism: A preface. In H. Foster (Ed.), *The anti-aesthetic: Essays on postmodern culture* (pp. ix–xvi). Port Townsend, Wash.: Bay Press.

Foucault, M. (1979a). *Discipline and punish: The birth of the prison* (A. Sheridan, Trans.). New York: Vintage. (Original work published 1975.)

———(1979b). What is an author? In J. V. Harari (Ed.), *Textual Strategies* (pp. 141–60). Ithaca, N.Y.: Cornell University Press.

———(1980). *Power/knowledge: Selected interviews and other writings 1972–1977.* New York: Pantheon.

———(1984). *The Foucault reader.* P. Rabinow (Ed.). New York: Pantheon Books.

———(1988). The ethic of care for the self as a practice of freedom. (1984 interview.) In J. Bernauer & D. Rasmussen (Eds.), *The final Foucault* (pp. 1–20). Cambridge, Mass: MIT Press.

Fox, N., & Fein, G. (1988). Infant day care: A special issue. *Early Childhood Research Quarterly* 3 (3): 227–234.

Franks, D. D., & McCarthy, E. D. (Eds.). (1989). *The Sociology of emotions: Original essays.* Greenwich, Conn: JAI.

Fraser, N. (1989). *Unruly practices: Power, discourse and gender in contemporary social theory.* Minneapolis: University of Minnesota Press.

Fraser, N., & Nicholson, L. (1988). Social criticism without philosophy: An encounter between feminism and postmodernism. *Theory, Culture, and Society* 5: 373–94.

Freire, P. (1970). *Pedagogy of the oppressed* (M. B. Ramos, Trans.). New York: Seabury.

———(1985). *The politics of education: Culture, power and liberation.* South Hadley, Mass.: Bergin & Garvey.

Friedman, S. (1990). NICHD infant child-care network: The national study of young children's lives. *Zero to Three* 10 (3): 21–23.

Frye, D. (1982). The problem of infant day care. In E. Zigler & E. Gordon (Eds.), *Day care: Scientific and social policy issues* (pp. 223–51). Boston: Auburn House.

Gabarino, J.; Stott, F.; & the Faculty of the Erikson Institute. (1989). *What children can tell us: Eliciting, interpreting, and evaluating information from children.* San Francisco: Jossey Bass.

Gadamer, H. G. (1975). *Truth and method.* New York: Seabury. (Original work published 1960.)

———(1976). *Philosophical hermeneutics.* Berkeley: University of California.

Galinsky, E., & Phillips, D. (1988, November). The day care debate. *Parents Magazine: 113–15.*

Galluzzo, D.; Matheson, C.; Moore, J.; & Howes, C. (1988). Social orientation to peers in infant child care. *Early Childhood Research Quarterly* 3 (4): 403–16.

Gamble, T., & Zigler, E. (1986). Effects of infant day care: Another look at the evidence. *American Journal of Orthopsychiatry* 56 (1): 26–42.

Gatens, M. (1986). Feminism, philosophy and riddles without answers. In C. Pateman & E. Gross (Eds.), *Feminist challenges: Social and political theory* (pp. 13–29). Boston: Northeastern University Press.

Geertz, C. (1973). *The interpretation of cultures: Collected essays.* New York: Basic.

Genishi, C. (1982). Observational research methods for early childhood education. In B. Spodek (Ed.), *Handbook of research in early childhood education* (pp. 564–91). New York: The Free Press.

Gilligan, C. (1982). *In a different voice: Psychological theory and women's development.* Cambridge: Harvard University Press.

———(1988). Remapping the moral domain: New images of self in relationship. In C. Gilligan, J. Ward, J. Taylor, & B. Bardige (Eds.), *Mapping the moral domain* (pp. 3–19). Cambridge, Mass.: Harvard University Press.

Gilligan, C., & Wiggins, G. (1988). The origins of morality in early child-hood relationships. In C. Gilligan, J. Ward, J. Taylor, & B. Bardige (Eds.), *Mapping the moral domain* (pp. 111–38). Cambridge, Mass.: Harvard University Press.

Gintis, H. (1972). Alienation and power. *The Review of Radical Political Economics* 4 (5): 1–34.

Giroux, H. (1981). *Ideology, culture, and the process of schooling.* Philadelphia: Temple University.

———(1987). Citizenship, public philosophy, and the struggle for democracy. *Educational Theory* 37 (2): 103–20.

———(1991a). Modernism, postmodernism, and feminism: Rethinking the boundaries of educational discourse. In H. Giroux (Ed.), *Postmodernism, feminism and cultural politics* (pp. 1–59). Albany, N.Y.: State University of New York Press.

———(1991b). Postmodernism as border pedagogy: Redefining the boundaries of race and ethnicity. In H. Giroux (Ed.), *Postmodernism, feminism and cultural politics* (pp. 217–56). Albany, N.Y.: State University of New York Press.

Glickman, B., & Springer, N. (1978). *Who cares for the baby? Choices in child care.* New York: Schocken.

Goffman, E. (1959). *The presentation of self in everyday life.* New York: Doubleday.

———(1961). *Asylums: Essays in the social situation of mental patients and other inmates.* Garden City, N.Y.: Anchor Books/Doubleday.

———(1967). *Interaction ritual: Essays on face-to- face behavior.* New York: Pantheon Books/Random House.

Gonzalez-Mena, J., & Eyer, D. W. (1993). *Infants, toddlers, and their care-givers.* Mountain View, Calif.: Mayfield.

Gordon, S. L. (1981). The sociology of sentiments and emotions. In M. Rosenberg & R. H. Turner (Eds.), *Social psychology: Sociological perspectives* (pp. 562–92). New York: Basic.

———(1985). Micro-sociological theories of emotion. In H. J. Helle & S. N. Eisenstadt (Eds.), *Micro-sociological theory: Perspectives on sociological theory, vol. 2* (pp. 133–47). Beverly Hills, Calif.: Sage.

———(1989a). The socialization of children's emotions: Emotional culture, competence, and exposure. In C. Saarni & P. L. Harris (Eds.), *Children's understandings of emotions* (pp. 319–49). Cambridge, Mass.: Cambridge University Press.

———(1989b). Institutional and impulsive orientations in selectively appropriating emotions to self. In D. D. Franks & E. D. McCarthy

(Eds.), *The sociology of emotions: Original essays* (pp. 115–35). Greenwich, Conn.: JAI.

Graham, H. (1983). Caring: A labour of love. In J. Finch & D. Groves (Eds.), *A labour of love: Women, work and caring* (pp. 13-30). Boston, Mass: Routledge & Kegan Paul.

Grimshaw, J. (1986). *Philosophy and feminist thinking*. Minneapolis: University of Minnesota Press.

Grubb, W. N., & Lazerson, M. (1982). *Broken promises: How Americans fail their children*. New York: Basic.

Guba, E., & Lincoln, Y. (1982). Epistemological and methodological bases of naturalistic inquiry. *Educational Communication and Technology Journal* 30 (4): 233–52.

Guttentag, R. (1987). From another perspective. *Zero to Three* 8 (2): 21.

Habermas, J. (1971). *Knowledge and human interests* (J. J. Shapiro, Trans.). Boston: Beacon Press. (Original work published in 1968.)

Hall, S. (1980). Cultural studies and the centre: Some problematics and problems. In S. Hall (Ed.), *Culture, media, language: Working papers in cultural studies, 1972–1979*. Hutchinson, Canada: The Centre for Contemporary Cultural Studies, University of Birmingham.

Harding, S., (Ed.). (1987). *Feminism and methodology*. Bloomington, Ind.: Indiana University.

Harkness, S., & Super, C. (1983). The cultural construction of child development: A framework for the socialization of affect. *Ethos* 11 (4): 221–31.

Harre, R. (Ed.). (1986). *The social construction of emotions*. Oxford: Basil Blackwell.

Hartley, R., & Goldenson, R. M. (1963). *The complete book of children's play*. New York: Crowell Co.

Harvey, D. (1989). *The condition of postmodernity: An inquiry into the origins of cultural change*. Cambridge, Mass.: Basil Blackwell.

Hatch, J. A. (1993). Ethical conflicts in a study of peer stigmatization in kindergarten. Paper presented at the annual meeting of the American Educational Research Association, Atlanta.

Heidegger, M. (1962). *Being and time*. New York: Harper & Row. (Original work published 1927.)

———(1982). *The basic problems of phenomenology*. Bloomington: Indiana University.

Hein, H. (1987, November). The feminist challenge to science. *American Philosophical Association Newsletter on Feminism and Philosophy*.

Hill, T. E. (1987). The importance of autonomy. In E. Kittay & D. Meyers (Eds.), *Women and moral theory* (pp. 129–38). Totowa, N.J.: Rowman & Littlefield.

Hirsh, A. (1982). *The French new left*. Montreal: Black.

Hochschild, A. R. (1979). Emotion work, feeling rules, and social structure. *American Journal of Sociology* 85: 551–75.

———(1983). *The managed heart: The commercialization of human feeling*. Berkeley: University of California.

Hofferth, S., & Phillips, D. A. (1987). Child care in the United States 1970–1995. *Journal of Marriage and Family* 49: 559–71.

Hoffman, L. (1984). Maternal employment and the young child. In M. Perlmutter (Ed.), *Parent-child interaction and parent-child relations in child development* (pp. 101–27). Hillsdale, N.J.: Lawrence Erlbaum Associates.

Howard, G. S. (1983). Toward methodological pluralism. *Journal of Counseling Psychology* 30 (1): 19–21.

Howes, C. (1987). Quality indicators in infant and toddler child care: The Los Angeles study. In D. Phillips (Ed.), *Quality in child care: What does the research tell us?* (pp. 81–88). Washington, D.C.: National Association for the Education of Young Children.

———(1989). Research in review: Infant child care. *Young Children* 44 (6): 24–28.

Hoy, D. C. (1988). Foucault: Modern or postmodern? In J. Arac (Ed.), *After Foucault: Humanistic knowledge, postmodern challenges* (pp. 12–41). New Brunswick: Rutgers University.

Husserl, E. (1962). *Ideas: General introduction to a pure phenomenology*. New York: Collier. (Original work published 1913.)

———(1970). *The idea of phenomenology*. The Hague: Martinus Nijhoff.

Huyssen, A. (1984). Mapping the postmodern. *New German Critique* 33: 5–51.

James, W. (1981). *Pragmatism*. Indianapolis: Hackett Publishing. (Original work published 1907.)

Jameson, F. (1984). The politics of theory: Ideological positions in the postmodernism debate. *New German Critique* 33: 53–65.

Jay, M. (1973). *The dialectical imagination: A history of the Frankfurt School and the Institute of Social Research, 1923–1950*. Boston: Little, Brown.

Jersild, A. (1955). *When teachers face themselves*. New York: Teachers College, Columbia University.

Johnson, E. (1990). The value of noise and confusion. *Education Week* 9: (33).

Jones, K. B. (1988). On authority: Or, why women are not entitled to speak. In I. Diamond & L. Quinby (Eds.), *Feminism and Foucault*: *Reflections on resistance* (pp. 119–13). Boston: Northeastern University Press.

Jones, L. (1985). Father-infant relations in the first year of life. In M. Hanson & F. Bozett (Eds.), *Dimensions of fatherhood* (pp. 93–114). Beverly Hills, Calif.: Sage.

Kagan, J. (1979). Family experience and the child's development. *American Psychologist* 34: 886–91.

———(1981). *The second year*. Cambridge, Mass.: Harvard University Press.

———(1984). *The nature of the child*. New York: Basic.

———(1987). Perspectives on infancy. In J. Osofsky (Ed.), *Handbook of infant development* (2d ed.) (pp. 1150–98). New York: John Wiley & Sons, Inc.

Kagan, J.; Kearsley, R.; & Zelazo, P. (1980). *Infancy: Its place in human development*. Cambridge: Harvard University Press.

Kanter, R. M. (1975). Women and the structure of organizations: Explorations in theory and behavior. In M. Millman & R. M. Kanter (Eds.), *Another voice: Feminist perspectives on social life and social science* (pp. 34–74). New York: Anchor Books.

Karen, R. (1990). Becoming attached. *The Atlantic Monthly* 265 (2): 35–70.

Katz, L. (1980). Mothering and teaching—Some significant distinctions. In L. Katz (Ed.), *Current topics in early childhood education, vol. 3* (pp. 47–63). Norwood, N.J.: Ablex.

Kellner, D. (1991). Reading images critically: Toward a postmodern pedagogy. In H. Giroux (Ed.), *Postmodernism, feminism, and cultural politics* (pp. 60–82). Albany, N.Y.: State University of New York Press.

Keohane, N.; Rosaldo, M.; & Gelpi, B. (Eds.) (1981). *Feminist theory: A critique of ideology*. Chicago: University of Chicago.

Kilmer, S. (1979). Infant-toddler group day care: A review of research. In L. Katz (Ed.), *Current topics in early childhood education, vol. 2* (pp. 69–115). Norwood, N.J.: Ablex.

Klein, J. T. (1989). Teaching and mother love. *Educational Theory* 39 (4): 373–83.

Kohlberg, L., & Mayer, R. (1972). Development as the aim of education. *Harvard Educational Review* 42 (4): 449–96.

Kontos, S., & Stremmel, A. (1988). Caregivers' perceptions of working conditions in a child care environment. *Early Childhood Research Quarterly* 3 (1): 77–90.

Kuykendall, E. (1983). Toward an ethic of nurturance: Luce Irigaray on mothering and power. In J. Trebilcot (Ed.), *Mothering: Essays in feminist theory* (pp. 263–74). Totowa, N.J.: Rowman & Allenheld.

Lamb, M. (Ed.) (1976). *The role of the father in child development.* New York: Wiley.

———(1982). Maternal employment and child development: A review. In M. Lamb (Ed.), *Nontraditional families: Parenting and child development* (pp. 45–69). Hillsdale, N.J.: Lawrence Erlbaum.

Lather, P. (1986). Research as praxis. *Harvard Educational Review* 56 (3): 257–77.

———(1991). Deconstructing/deconstructive inquiry: The politics of knowing and being known. *Educational Theory* 41 (2): 143–73.

Leach, M., & Page, R. (1987, May/June). Why home economics should be morally biased. *Illinois Teacher:* 169–74.

Leavitt, R. L. (1993a). Studying children in day care: Personal reflections and dilemmas. Paper presented at the annual meeting of the American Educational Research Association, Atlanta.

———(1993b). Conversations with caregivers: An inquiry into the work of caregiving. Unpublished research proposal.

Leavitt, R. L., & Eheart, B. K. (1985). *Toddler day care: A guide to responsive caregiving.* Lexington, Mass.: D.C. Heath.

Leavitt, R. L., & Power, M. B. (1989). Emotional socialization in the postmodern era: Children in day care. *Social Psychology Quarterly* 52 (1): 35–43.

Lewin, M. (Ed.). (1984). *In the shadow of the past: Psychology portrays the sexes.* New York: Columbia University.

Lewis, M. (1987). Social development in infancy and early childhood. In J. Osofsky (Ed.), *Handbook of infant development* (2d ed.) (pp. 419–493). New York: John Wiley & Sons, Inc.

Lewis, M., & Saarni, C. (Eds.). (1985). *The socialization of emotions.* New York: Plenum Press.

Lieberman, A. (1991). Attachment and exploration: The toddler's dilemma. *Zero to Three* 11 (3): 6–11.

Lief, H. I., & Fox, R.C. (1963). Training for "detached concern" in medical students. In H.I. Lief, V.F. Lief, & N. R. Lief (Eds.), *The psychological basis of medical practice* (pp. 12–35). New York: Harper & Row.

Liljestrom, R. (1983). The public child, the commercial child, and our child. In F. S. Kessel & A. W. Siegel (Eds.), *The child and other cultural inventions* (pp. 124–52). New York: Praeger.

Loseke, D. (1989). If only my mother lived down the street. In J. M. Henslin (Ed.), *Marriage and family in a changing society* (pp. 317–28). New York: Free Press.

Loseke, D. R., & Cahill, S. E. (no date). Trust and suspicion in daycare transactions. (Unpublished manuscript.)

Love, B., & Shanklin, E. (1983). The answer is matriarchy. In J. Trebilcot (Ed.), *Mothering: Essays in feminist theory* (pp. 275–83). New Jersey: Rowman & Allanheld.

Lyotard, J. (1984). *The postmodern condition: A report on knowledge* (G. Bennington & B. Massumi, Trans.). Minneapolis: University of Minnesota. (Original work published 1979.)

Madison, G. B. (1990). *The hermeneutics of postmodernity.* Bloomington, Ind.: Indiana University.

Manen, M. V. (1984). Practicing phenomenological writing. *Phenomenology and Pedagogy* 2 (1): 36–69.

———(1990). *Researching lived experience: Human science for an action sensitive pedagogy.* London; Ontario, Canada: The University of Western Ontario.

Martin, J. R. (1988). Science in a different style. *American Philosophical Quarterly* 25 (2): 129–40.

Martinez, S. (1989). Child care and federal policy. In J. Lande, S. Scarr, & N. Gunzenhauser (Eds.), *Caring for children: Challenge to America* (pp. 111–28). Hillsdale, N.J.: Lawrence Erlbaum.

Marx, K. (1983). Alienated labor. In E. Kamenka (Ed.), *The portable Karl Marx* (pp. 131–46). New York: Viking Penguin. (Original work published in 1844.)

Maslach, C., & Pines, A. (1977). The burnout syndrome in the day care setting. *Child Care Quarterly* 6 (2): 100–13.

McCartney, K., & Phillips, D. (1988). Motherhood and child care. In B. Birns & D. Hay (Eds.), *The different faces of motherhood* (pp. 157–83). New York: Plenum Press.

McLaren, P. (1986). Postmodernity and the death of politics: A Brazilian reprieve. *Educational Theory* 36 (4): 389–401.

———(1989). *Life in schools: An introduction to critical pedagogy in the foundations of education.* New York: Longman.

———(1991). Schooling the postmodern body: critical pedagogy and the politics of enfleshment. In H. Giroux (Ed.), *Postmodernism, femi-*

nism, and cultural politics (pp. 60–82). Albany, N.Y.: State University of New York Press.

Mead, G. H. (1907). The educational situation in the Chicago Public Schools. *The City Club Bulletin* 1.

——(1962). *Mind, self and society.* Chicago: University of Chicago. (Original work published 1934.)

Merleau-Ponty, M. (1962). *The phenomenology of perception.* London: Routledge & Kegan Paul.

——(1964). *The primacy of perception* (J. M. Edie, Trans.). Evanston: Northwestern University.

Meyers, D. (1987). The socialized individual and individual autonomy. In E. Kittay & D. Meyers (Eds.), *Women and moral theory* (pp. 139-53). Totowa, N.J.: Rowman & Littlefield.

Mills, C. W. (1959). *The sociological imagination.* New York: Oxford University.

Miringhoff, N. (1987). A timely and controversial article. *Zero to Three* 7 (3): 26.

Misgeld, D., & Jardine, D. (1989). Hermeneutics as the undisciplined child: Hermeneutic and technical images of education. In M. Packer & R. Addison (Eds.), *Entering the circle: Hermeneutic investigation in psychology* (pp. 259–73). Albany: State University of New York Press.

Modigliani, K. (1986). But who will take care of the children? Child care, women, and devalued labor. *Journal of Education* 168 (3): 46–69.

Morris, M. (1988). Introduction: Feminism, reading, postmodernism. In M. Morris (Ed.), *The pirates fiancee: Feminism, reading, postmodernism* (pp. 1–23). London: Verso.

Morrison, H. (1988). *The seven gifts: A new view of teaching inspired by the philosophy of Maurice Merleau- Ponty.* Chicago: Educational Studies Press.

Neugebauer, R. (1989). Surveying the landscape: A look at child care '89. *Child Care Information Exchange* 66: 13–16.

New, C., & David, M. (1985). Introduction. In C. New & M. David (Eds.), *For the children's sake: Making child care more than women's business* (pp. 13–24). New York: Penguin Books.

New, R. (1990). Excellent early education: A city in Italy has it. *Young Children* 45 (6): 4–10.

Nicholson, C. (1989). Postmodernism, feminism, and education: The need for solidarity. *Educational Theory* 39 (3): 197–205.

Noddings, N. (1984). *Caring: A feminine approach to ethics and moral education.* Berkeley: University of California.

————(1992). *The challenge to care in schools*. New York: Teachers College Press.

Oakley, A. (1986). Feminism, motherhood, and medicine—who cares? In J. Mitchell & A. Oakley (Eds.), *What is feminism?* (pp. 127–50). Oxford: Basil Blackwell.

Owens, C. (1983). The discourse of others: Feminists and postmodernism. In H. Foster (Ed.), *The anti-aesthetic: Essays on postmodernist culture* (pp. 57–82). Port Townsend, Wash: Bay Press.

Packer, M. (1985). Hermeneutic inquiry in the study of human conduct. *American Psychologist* 40 (10): 1081–93.

————(1987). *Interpretive research and social development in developmental psychology*. Paper presented at the Biennial Meeting of the Society for Research in Child Development, Baltimore, Md.

Packer, M., & Addison, R. (1989a). Introduction. In M. Packer & R. Addison (Eds.), *Entering the circle: Hermeneutic investigation in psychology* (pp. 13–36). Albany: State University of New York Press.

————(1989b). Evaluating an interpretive account. In M. Packer & R. Addison (Eds.), *Entering the circle: Hermeneutic investigation in psychology* (pp. 275–92). Albany: State University of New York Press.

Packer, M., & Mergendollar, J. (1989). The development of practical social understanding in elementary school-age children. In L. T. Winegar (Ed.), *Social interaction and the development of children's understanding* (pp. 67–94). Norwood, N.J.: Ablex.

Parke, R. (1979). Emerging themes for social-emotional development. *American Psychologist* 34 (10): 930–31.

Pateman, C., & Gross, E. (1986). *Feminist challenges: Social and political theory*. Boston: Northeastern University.

Pawl, J. (1990a). Infants in day care: Reflections on experiences, expectations and relationships. *Zero to Three* 10 (3): 1–6.

————(1990b). Attending to the emotional well being of children, families and caregivers: Contributions of infant mental health specialists to child care. *Zero to Three* 10 (3): 7.

Phillips, D. (1987a, November). Infants and child care: The new controversy. *Child Care Information Exchange* 19–22.

————(1987b). Epilogue. In D. Phillips (Ed.), *Quality in child care: What does the research tell us?* (pp. 121–26). Washington, D. C.: National Association for the Education of Young Children.

Phillips, D. A.; McCartney, D.; Scarr, S.; & Howes, S. (1987). Selective review of infant day care: A cause for concern. *Zero to Three* 7 (3): 18–21.

Philp, M. (1985). Michel Foucault. In Q. Skinner (Ed.), *The return of grand theory in the human sciences* (pp. 65–81). Cambridge: Cambridge University Press.

Piers, M. (1989). Foreword. In J. Gabarino, F. Stott, and the Faculty of The Erikson Institute (Eds.), *What children can tell us: Eliciting, interpreting, and evaluating information from children* (pp. xi–xiv). San Francisco: Jossey-Bass.

Polakow, V. (1992). *The erosion of childhood.* Chicago: University of Chicago Press.

Polkinghorne, D. (1983). *Methodology for the human sciences.* Albany: State University of New York Press.

Porter, C., & Potenza, A. (1983). Alternative methodologies for early childhood research. In S. Kilmer (Ed.), *Advances in early education and day care, vol. 3* (pp. 155–86). Greenwich, Conn.: JAI.

Power, M. B. (1985a). The child's emotionality: A naturalistic investigation. Unpublished doctoral dissertation, Urbana: University of Illinois.

———(1985b). The ritualization of emotional conduct in early childhood. In N. K. Denzin (Ed.), *Studies in symbolic interaction, vol. 6* (pp. 213–27). Greenwich, Conn.: JAI.

———(1986). Socializing of emotionality in early childhood: The influence of emotional essociates. In P. Adler & P. Adler (Eds.), *Sociological studies of child development, vol. 1* (pp. 259-82). Greenwich, Conn: JAI.

———(1987). *Interpretive interactionism and early childhood socialization.* Paper presented at the Stone SSSI Symposium, Urbana, Ill.

Rabinow, P., & Sullivan, W. (Eds.). (1979). *Interpretive social science: A reader.* Berkeley: University of California Press.

Reynolds, E. (1990). *Guiding young children: A child centered approach.* Mountain View, Calif.: Mayfield.

Rhodes, S. L. (1979). Trends in child development research important to day care policy. *Social Service Review* 53: 284–94.

Rose, H. (1986). Women's work: Women's knowledge. In J. Mitchell & A. Oakley (Eds.), *What is feminism?* (pp. 151–83). Oxford:Basil Blackwell.

Roth, P. (1987). *Meaning and method in the social sciences: A case for methodological pluralism.* Ithaca, N.Y.: Cornell University Press.

Rousseau, J. (1979). *Emile* (A. Bloom, Trans.). New York: Basic Books. (Original work published 1762.)

Rubenstein, J. (1985). The effects of maternal employment on young children. *Applied Developmental Psychology* 2: 99–128.

Rubenstein, J., & Howes, C. (1983). Social-emotional development of toddlers in day care: The role of peers and of individual differences. In S. Kilmer (Ed.), *Advances in early education and day care, vol. 3* (pp. 13–45). Greenwich, Conn.: JAI.

Ruddick, S. (1983). Maternal thinking. In J. Trebilcot (Ed.), *Mothering: Essays in feminist theory* (pp. 213–230). Totowa, N.J.: Rowman & Allenheld.

———(1987). Remarks on the sexual politics of reason. In E. Kittay & D. Meyers (Eds.), *Women and moral theory* (pp. 237–60). Totowa, N.J.: Rowman & Littlefield.

———(1989). *Maternal thinking: Toward a politics of peace.* Boston: Beacon Press.

Rutter, M. (1981). *Maternal deprivation reassessed.* New York: Penguin.

Ryan, M. (1982). *Marxism and deconstruction: A critical articulation.* Baltimore: Johns Hopkins University.

Saarni, C. (1989). Children's understanding and strategic control of emotional expression in social transactions. In C. Saarni & P. L. Harris (Eds.), *Children's understanding of emotion* (pp. 181–208). Cambridge: Cambridge University Press.

Saarni, C., & Harris, P. (Eds.). (1989). *Children's understandings of emotions.* Cambridge, Mass.: Cambridge University Press.

Sartre, J. P. (1956). *Being and nothingness.* (H. E. Barnes, Trans.). New York: Simon & Schuster. (Original work published 1943.)

———(1962). *Sketch for a theory of the emotions* (P. Mariet, Trans.). London: Methuen. (Original work published 1939.)

———(1963). *Search for a method* (H. E. Barnes, Trans.). New York: Knopf. (Original work published 1960.)

———(1976). *Critique of dialectical reason* (A. Sheridan-Smith, Trans.). London: NLP. (Original work published 1960.)

———(1981). The family idiot: Gustave Flaubert, 1821–1857 (C. Cosman, Trans.). Chicago: University of Chicago Press. (Original work published 1971.)

Sawicki, J. (1988). Feminism and the power of Foucaldian [sic] discourse. In J. Arac (Ed.), *After Foucault: humanistic knowledge, postmodern challenges* (pp. 161–78). New Brunswick: Rutgers University.

Scarr, S. (1979). Psychology and children: Current research and practice. *American Psychologist* 34 (10): 809–11.

Schon, D. (1983). *The reflective practitioner.* New York: Basic.

Scheler, M. (1970). *The nature of sympathy* (P. Heath, Trans.). Hamden, Conn.: Archon Books, Shoe String Press. (Original work published 1913.)

Schroeder, W. R. (1984). *Sartre and his predecessors*. London: Routledge & Kegan Paul.

Schutz, A. (1967). *The phenomenology of the social world*. Evanston: Northwestern University Press.

Schutz, A., & Luckmann, T. (1973). *The structures of the life world, vol. 1* (R. Zaner & H. T. Englehardt, Jr., Trans.). Evanston: Northwestern University Press

Schwalbe, M. (1986). *The psychosocial consequences of alienated labor*. Albany: State University of New York Press.

Shalin, D. N. (1986). Pragmatism and social interactionism. *American Sociological Review* 51: 9–29.

Shanok, R. S. (1990). Parenthood: A process marking identity and intimacy capacities. *Zero to Three* 11 (2): 1–9.

Sharron, A. (1982). Dimensions of time. In N. K. Denzin (Ed.), *Studies in symbolic interaction, vol. 4* (pp. 63–89). Greenwich, Conn: JAI.

Shaull, R. (1970). Introduction. In P. Freire, *Pedagogy of the oppressed*. New York: Seabury.

Shell, E. R. (1988). Babes in day care. *The Atlantic* 262 (2): 73–74.

Shields, S., & Koster, B. (1989). Emotional stereotyping of parents in child-rearing manuals, 1915-1980. *Social Psychology Quarterly* 52 (1): 44–55.

Shott, S. (1979). Emotion and social life: A symbolic interactionist analysis. *American Journal of Sociology* 84: 1317–34.

Silberman, C. (1970). *Crisis in the classroom*. New York: Random House.

Silvers, R. (1983). On the other side of silence. *Human Studies* 6: 91–108.

Smith, D. E. (1979). A sociology for women. In J. A. Sherman & E. T. Beck (Eds.), *The prism of sex: Essays in the sociology of knowledge* (pp. 135–87). Madison: University of Wisconsin Press.

———(1987). *The everyday world as problematic*. Boston: Northestern University Press.

Smith, H., & Robbins, A. (1982). Structured ethnography: The study of parental involvement. *American Behavioral Scientist* 26 (1): 45–61.

Smith, J. F. (1983). Parenting and property. In J. Trebilcot (Ed.), *Mothering: Essays in feminist theory* (pp. 199–212). Totowa, N.J.: Rowman & Allenheld.

Smith, J. K. (1984, Winter). The problem of criteria for judging interpretive inquiry. *Educational evaluation and policy analysis* 6 (4): 379–91.

Smith, J. K., & Heshusius, L. (1986). Closing down the conversation: The end of the quantitative-qualitative debate among educational inquirers. *Educational Researcher* 15 (1): 4–12.

Smith, P. (1990). Feminist jurisprudence. *American Philosophical Association Newsletter on Philosophy and Law* 90 (1): 152–59.

Snow, C. (1989). *Infant development.* Englewood Cliffs, N.J.: Prentice Hall.

Sommerville, C. J. (1990). *The rise and fall of childhood.* New York: Vintage Books, Random House.

Stanley, L., & Wise, S. (1983). *Breaking out: Feminist consciousness and feminist research.* London: Routledge, Kegan, & Paul.

Steele, R. (1989). A critical hermeneutics for psychology: Beyond positivism to an exploration of the textual unconscious. In M. Packer & R. Addison (Eds.), *Entering the circle: Hermeneutic investigation in psychology* (pp. 223–37). Albany: State University of New York Press.

Steele, S. (1990). The "unseen agent" of low self-esteem. *Education Week* 10 (5): 36.

Steinfels, M. (1973). *Who's minding the children? The history and politics of day care in America.* New York: Simon & Schuster.

Stuhr, J. (1990). Subjects constructed, deconstructed, and reconstructed. *The Journal of Philosophy* 90: 656–57.

Sullivan, H. S. (1953). *The interpersonal of psychiatry.* New York: Norton.

Suransky, V. Polakow (1977). *The erosion of childhood: A social phenomenological study of early institutionalization.* Unpublished doctoral dissertation, Ann Arbor: University of Michigan.

———(1983). Tales of rebellion and resistance: The landscape of early instutional life. *Journal of Education* 165 (2): 135–57.

Tesch, R. (1985). *Human science research bibliography.* P.O. Box 30070, Santa Barbara, Calif.

Thompson, R. (1987). Attachment theory and day care research. *Zero to Three* 8 (2): 19–20.

———(1988). The effects of infant day care through the prism of attachment theory: A critical appraisal. *Early Childhood Research Quarterly* 3 (3): 273–81.

Treichler, P. (1986). Teaching feminist theory. In C. Nelson (Ed.), *Theory in the classroom* (pp. 57–128). Urbana: University of Illinois.

Tyler, S. A. (1986). Postmodern ethnography: From document of the occult to occult document. In J. Clifford & G. Marcus (Eds.), *Writing culture: The poetics and politics of ethnography* (pp. 122–40). Berkeley, Calif.: University of California Press.

Vandenberg, B. (1987a, April). *Development within an existential framework*. Paper presented at the Society for Research in Child Development meeting, Baltimore, Md.

———(1987b, April). *Developmental psychology and the death of god*. Paper presented at the Society for Research in Child Development meeting, Baltimore, Md.

Vandenberg, D. (1971). *Being and education*. Englewood Cliffs, N.J.: Prentice-Hall.

Waksler, F. (1986). Studying children: phenomenological insights. *Human Studies* 9: 71–82.

Wallis, C. (1987, June 22). Is day care bad for babies? *Time Magazine*: 54–63.

Walsh, D.; Baturka, N.; Smith, E.; & Cotter, N. (1989, September). *Changing one's mind—Maintaining one's identity: A first grade teacher's story*. Paper presented at the Qualitative Research in Early Childhood Settings Symposium, Knoxville, Tenn.

Warren, S. (1984). *The emergence of dialectical theory*. Chicago: University of Chicago Press.

Wartofsky, M. (1983). The child's construction of the world and the world's construction of the child: From historical epistemology to historical psychology. In F. Kessel & A. Siegel (Eds.), *The child and other cultural inventions* (pp. 188–215). New York: Praeger.

Weber, M. (1962). *Basic concepts in sociology* (H. P Secher, Trans.). Secaucus, N.J.: Citadel.

Weinrub, M.; Jaeger, E.; & Hoffman L. (1988). Predicting infant outcomes in families of employed and nonemployed mothers. *Early Childhood Research Quarterly* 3 (4): 361–78.

White, B. (1981, November). Viewpoint: Should you stay home with your baby? *Young Children*: 11–17.

White, B., & Watts, J. (1973). *Experience and environment, vol. 1*. Englewood Cliffs, N.J.: Prentice Hall.

White, S. (1983). Psychology as a moral science. In F. Kessel & A. Siegel (Eds.), *The child and other cultural inventions* (pp. 1–25). New York: Praeger.

Whitebook, M.; Howes, C.; Darrah, R.; & Friedman, J. (1982). Caring for the caregivers: Staff burnout in child care. In L. Katz (Ed.), *Current topics in early childhood education, vol. 4*. (pp. 211–35). Norwood, N.J.: Ablex.

Whitebook, M.; Howes, C.; & Phillips, D. (1989). *Who cares? Child care teachers and the quality of care in America. Final report: National child care staffing study*. Oakland, Calif.: Child CareEmployee Project.

Willard, A. (1988). Cultural scripts for mothering. In C. Gilligan; J. Ward; J. Taylor; & B. Bardige (Eds.), *Mapping the moral domain* (pp. 225–43). Cambridge, Mass.: Harvard University Press.

Willis, A., & Ricciuti, H. (1975). *A good beginning for babies: Guidelines for group care*. Washington, D.C.: The National Association for the Education of Young Children.

Wingert, P., & Kantrowitz, B. (1990, Winter/Spring special edition). The day care generation. *Newsweek: 86–92.*

Yarrow, L. (1979). *Emotional development. American Psychologist* 34 (10): 951–57.

Young, R. (1981). Post-structuralism: An introduction. In R. Young (Ed.), *Untying the text*. Baltimore: Johns Hopkins University.

Zigler, E., & Lang, M. (1991). *Child care choices: Balancing the needs of children, families, and society*. New York: The Free Press.

Zimiles, H. (1986). Rethinking the role of research: New issues and lingering doubts in an era of expanding preschool education. *Early Childhood Research Quarterly* 1 (3): 189–206.

Index

Activities, daily: adult-directed, 30; adult support for, 77; children's initiation of, 32, 37–38; custodial nature of, 30
Alienation, 17, 23, 51, 54, 61, 63, 64, 69, 111$n6$, 112$n9$
Anger, expressing, 13, 57
Anti-self, 67
Attachment: and autonomy, 3; insecure, 11; insecure-avoidant, 7; mother-child, 6–8; to primary caregiver, 6; theory, 6–8, 10, 11, 12
Autonomy, 13, 22, 23, 24, 70, 71, 78, 92; and attachment, 3; caregivers', 47, 63; constructed definitions of, 3; development of, 3, 11, 40, 42; personal, 42; and repression of resistance, 40

Behavior: children's understanding of, 35; developmental explanation for, 57; learning, 19; self-directed, 18; surface, 58; symbolic, 17–18
Biting, 57
Bond, mother-child, 8–11, 21

Caregivers: adherence to schedules, 33; alienation of children, 51; attachment to, 6; autonomy of, 47, 63; burnout in, 63, 87; caring for, 88–89, 93, 97–99; center constraints on, 63; child-awareness of, 85–86; comforting responsibility of, 55, 59; control as primary goal of, 42; in decision-making process, 63; emotional alienation of, 65; in emotional culture, 2; emotional disengagement of, 60; emotional stress on, 61–63, 64, 87; empowerment of, 25; external preoccupation of, 53; inflexibility of, 47; isolation from adult society, 64; lack of awareness, 52; and language of gestures, 74; as meaning-makers, 24; need for control, 47, 48; objectification of children, 51; occupational hazards, 63–64; overinvolvement in activities, 37; power over children, 27–49, 91; professionalization of, 66, 88; protective boundaries provided by, 84; and restriction of iniative, 37; as time controllers, 34
Children: as becoming, 72, 112$n9$; capability for multiple relationships, 10, 11; compliance as goal, 32, 48; control of mobility of, 28, 29; daily schedules, 30–35; developmental needs, 96; and developmental power, 41; disciplinary time, 30–35; efforts at communication, 70; emotional control in, 58; emotional selves, 84; empowerment of, 2–3, 19, 25, 78, 84; expression of feelings, 57, 58; and extractive power, 41; insignificance of in day care, 67, 92; management precedence over being, 52; marginalization of, 23; as meaning-makers, 24, 25; objectification of, 51–60, 92; power of caregivers over, 27–49; regimentation of, 30–31; resistance to power, 38–41, 92; respect for, 70, 75, 77, 85; socialization of, 18, 19; use of force on, 41
Co-feeling, 76–77
Communication: adult-child, 75; caregiver-child, 53; children's efforts at, 70; development, 3; of disciplinary norms, 35; nonverbal, 18
Competence, 3, 11, 85

137